Boy Crazy

your
research
is incredible
necessary!!

- M. Peters

Boy Crazy

*Why Monogamy Is So Hard
for Gay Men and What
You Can Do About It*

Michael Shelton, MS, CAC

alyson books
NEW YORK

© 2008 by Michael Shelton

Manufactured in the United States of America

A trade paperback original published by Alyson Books
245 West 17th Street, New York, NY 10011
Distribution in the United Kingdom by Turnaround Publisher Services Ltd.
Unit 3, Olympia Trading Estate, Coburg Road, Wood Green
London N22 6TZ England

First Edition: November 2008

08 09 10 11 12 13 14 15 16 17 **a** 10 9 8 7 6 5 4 3 2 1

ISBN: 1-59350-071-8
ISBN-13: 978-1-59350-071-9

Library of Congress Cataloging-in-Publication data are on file.

Cover design by Victor Mingovits

FOR DONALD

Now you have a second book dedicated to you.

CONTENTS

PREFACE

I ENCOUNTERED a former colleague during the height of the holiday season, and, after trading estimates over how long it had been since we last saw each other, we decided to catch up over a quick coffee. As shoppers passed by our window, Gary informed me that he had made the "momentous" decision to become monogamous. He reminded me that monogamy had always seemed ridiculous and unnecessary to him; it was nothing more, in his past opinion at least, than a reluctant acceptance of the straight mating style that doesn't even work for heterosexual couples. But now he was ready. Anonymous sex, fuck buddies, and open relationships had left him feeling "empty" and in need of more. Nonmonogamy hadn't worked for him, and now he wanted to try monogamy. And by this he meant "strict monogamy" in which no outside sexual dalliances were allowable. All sexual activity now had to take place within the parameters of the relationship between him and his lover of two years.

Gary is a living example of a trend that I have noticed in the past several years: more and more gay male couples wholeheartedly endorsing voluntary monogamy. And I am not alone in my observation of the resurgence of monogamy; other professionals who work within the realms of either human sexuality or couples counseling have also noted this trend. Of course, during the height of the AIDS epidemic, optional monogamy reached an apex, but much of the motivation was based on the pragmatic desire to remain disease free. While disease considerations may still factor into a matrix of decision-making regarding monogamy versus nonmonogamy, the primary reason now is more romantic. Men believe that they will be more satisfied with their relationships and with their lives in general if they partake of a monogamous lifestyle.

Let it be clear at the onset that this book is not endorsing monogamy; in no way am I saying that gay men should be monogamous, that this relationship configuration is paramount over all others, and that only this type of relationship will bring lasting satisfaction. In fact, the second most frequent rejoinder I heard from men upon learning of my work was a reminder that not all gay men support or even desire monogamy. Monogamy, according to these men, is an unwanted vestige of a patriarchal and heterosexist mating system. Still, the most common response, even more common than diatribes against monogamy, were descriptions of frustrations, disappointment, and heartaches that came with monogamy attempts. Many gay men desire a long-term sexually committed relationship and keep trying for one in spite of previous failed attempts.

My original intent in writing this book was to detail how hardwired male sexuality makes long-term monogamy difficult for gay men. We have learned more about human sexuality in the past forty years than we have in our entire time on the planet, and we now know that all males face challenges with regard to monogamy. Gay men face additional challenges presented by gay culture, the dynamics of same-sex relations, and societal homophobia, but the similarities between gay and straight men are too evident and too profound to warrant merely a passing mention. Those readers who have been in relationships already know that monogamy is easy in the early stages of a relationship when passion rules. However, passion inevitably fades, and men experience, often suddenly, a longing for new lovers and new sexual experiences. This too is part of our hardwired sexuality; men, regardless of orientation, must navigate this often-torturous route.

But it is doubtful that long-term monogamy, defined here as remaining sexually exclusive with one person and one person alone for several years, is based on hardwired male sexuality alone. And indeed, when I analyzed the research, talked to experts in numerous fields touching upon monogamy (e.g., psychology, biology, couples therapy), examined the issue in the lives of my own clients, broached the topic with innumerable people—single gay men and those in couples—who had dealt with nonmonogamy, and, finally, pondered my own life, I found that there was much more influencing monogamy and gay men than my original and rather narrow focus on hardwired male sexuality. The picture is far more complex and nuanced than I had considered.

THERE ARE MANY REASONS for any gay man to examine the issue of monogamy. Perhaps a single gay man wants to know why it seems so hard to settle into a committed monogamous relationship; why do he and other gay men seem to find long-term monogamy so difficult? Others might already be in a long-term relationship but are experiencing an increasing temptation to engage in a brief, even anonymous, sexual fling. Maybe one partner suspects the other of sexual infidelity. It could even be that a couple has decided that they want to explore other relationship options; the highly erotic passion that sparked their relationship has diminished, and one or both men now seek out a method of maintaining their long-term commitment while simultaneously partaking of sexual novelty and excitement. This could range from negotiations over allowable external sexual dalliances to permanently including a third man in what will become a romantic triad. It is even possible that one partner is engaged in more than anonymous cruising or is now actively involved in a secret love affair with another man that is as meaningful as his relationship with his first lover.

Keeping all of these scenarios in mind, two questions frame this book. First, why is monogamy so challenging for gay men? Second, how do we make gay male relationships work if we know in advance that monogamy may (and likely will) eventually be an issue?

Many readers will intuitively acknowledge the forces affecting monogamy in their own relationships as they peruse the chapters of this book; some of these will hopefully begin to explore with their partner its relevance for their own relationship. Single men may proactively decide to approach new relationships with a more flexible perspective than the familiar marital model that has been inculcated into us since our childhoods or, conversely, the rigid and unbending antipathy toward monogamy so often promulgated in the gay community. Others—those I consider the romantics—will also read the information but scoff at its relevance for them. The romantic believes that long-term monogamy is likely, but he hasn't found the "right" person yet. For these men, this book will offer the latest research on maintaining monogamous relationships.

Finally, there will be those readers who have truly remained singularly and steadfastly monogamous while maintaining a healthy and loving relationship. They beat the odds, and their relationship is a model for many. Not all, of course, since, again, many gay men seethe at the thought of monogamy, and, as we will soon learn, monogamy might not even be an appropriate model for humans to base their love and sex lives upon. Still, many gay men want what these monogamous couples already have.

Introduction

MY DAWNING AWARENESS of the challenge that gay men have with monogamy began at a dinner party two decades ago. Ed and John, both in their early sixties, proudly informed other guests over the meal that they had been a couple for more than thirty years.

"Have you been monogamous the entire time?" a man in his midtwenties queried with obvious awe.

"Of course," Ed immediately responded.

"And if he wasn't, I would kill him," John added jokingly.

Several months later, I joined a new health club and quickly discovered that the facility's steam room was a popular spot for sexual activity. It was there that I encountered John once more. He didn't remember me as he removed his towel and stroked his semi-erect penis. I soon learned that John was no stranger to the regulars of the steam room. In fact, I was told that he gave the best oral sex in the place and had been an active initiator of sexual activity for years.

If research accurately reflects the reality of gay male relationships, most gay men either have already or will in the future engage in sexual activity with a person other than their partner. Studies find that the majority of gay men report sexual activity with another person outside of their relationship and that many keep this a secret. As for strict long-term monogamy in which there is absolutely no involvement with another sexual partner other than the man already in our lives, its presence is a rarity. These findings in no way minimize the challenges that lesbian and heterosexual couples also have with monogamy, but gay men experience the most difficulty by far.

Putting aside that admittedly sizable population of gay men that staunchly refuses to practice monogamy due to its heterosexual connotations, many still aspire to monogamy in a relationship. This aspiration, however, is thwarted when the reality of gay relationships intrudes. Single men wonder if they can maintain a long-term sexually committed relationship or question if they even want to make such a commitment when an unending variety of tempting sexual partners is so readily available. Similarly, these same men find it increasingly hard to believe that other gay men do indeed exist who also desire monogamy. For couples, one or both partners may struggle to maintain monogamy, especially as initial passion inevitably cools, and many will finally cross over from contemplation of sexual infidelity to outright action with an end result ranging from just one sexual tryst to many years of hidden dalliances. Additionally, it's certainly not uncommon for both partners to be actively engaged in furtive sexual activity, and many couples simply toss out the idea of monogamy altogether by agreeing to an "open" relationship.

Growing up as a gay male, I learned to take it for granted that gay men could not be monogamous. This unquestioned assumption arose based on statistics on gay male sexual activity, from the rhetoric of the political and religious right, from my gay male friends, and, unfortunately, from my own personal experiences in romantic relationships. Apparently a sizable portion of the gay male population holds this same belief. Polls and studies keep saying that gay men desire a monogamous relationship, but somehow or the other such relationships seem to elude us. A pertinent question then is "why?"

I was given the opportunity to ask just that question in 2006 while attending a series of seminars on gay relationships. During the second session, one of the participants, obviously still reeling from shock, confided that over the past week his lover of twelve years had been arrested after approaching an undercover law-enforcement officer for sexual activity in a local state park. This fellow attendee mistakenly thought that he and his partner had been monogamous. After a few sympathetic comments by other participants, I asked the entire group the obvious question: Why do you think monogamy is so difficult for gay men?

The answers that were given that night were the impetus for this book. Other than two men who admitted to having never been in a serious relationship, all other participants had monogamy-related experiences. Almost all could recount an episode in which either they or their partners (and on some occasions, both) failed at monogamy. Others wondered or outright suspected that their current partners were sexually unfaithful. And a third small group actively criticized the entire concept of monogamy. There were opinions, reasoned arguments, and personal testimonials as to the underlying factors interfering with gay male monogamy, but even the very best answers bordered on psychobabble and urban myth. There we were, seriously discussing an extremely relevant issue for the gay male community, and conjecture generated the best answers.

This book sets out to move past mere conjecture and instead to examine the true influences that make monogamy just so damn difficult for gay men.

A *Very* Brief Overview of the Research

In 2006, the American Psychological Association (APA) addressed the constitutionality of same-sex marriage. The good news is that the APA found that marriage bestows "substantial psychological, social, and health benefits" and should be an option for same-sex couples. But for those men who desire a monogamous relationship, there is bad news too: it could not determine whether a marriage (or any type of civil union or domestic partnership) would actually increase gay male monogamy.

Studies from the dawn of the AIDS era indicate that gay men tend to have a large number of sexual partners—even those who describe themselves as being invested in a committed relationship. Other studies give us even more detailed information about monogamy:

- *Gay males tend to become less monogamous the longer their relationship lasts. A recent study, however, throws some doubt on a common belief that most male couples are in a relationship for at least five years before they begin to explore additional sexual outlets. The median length of the current relationship in this study was a little more than two years; still, two-thirds of the men had sex with somebody else other than the primary partner.*
- *Many couples that claim to be monogamous do not take the definition of the word literally. Monogamy is interpreted as "emotional monogamy" and a commitment to be supportive through the travails of life, but this does not require sexual monogamy. Donald Symons, the renowned researcher*

who galvanized an interest in studying the similarities between gay and straight male sexuality, found that the majority of gay men eventually seek sexual activity with other men outside of their relationship with a partner. Still he marvels at their availability to remain emotionally monogamous in a long-term relationship in spite of outside sexual activity.

- *Many gay men have a highly restricted definition of monogamy: monogamy is maintained as long as anal sex does not occur with another person. Mutual masturbation, oral sex, and a host of other practices are allowable.*
- *Many gay men surreptitiously cheat on their partners.*

Research does indeed find that gay men have difficulty maintaining monogamy. Not all gay men of course, but certainly not a minority either. Still, many gay men claim to want a monogamous relationship. So why are we unsuccessful? We can ask the man in the street for his opinion, and indeed this is just what the first chapter of this book does. But for now, some of the common responses are that gay men are just "naturally" promiscuous, that there are too many available places for gay men to hook up for sex (gyms, parks, restrooms, and such), and that our inability to officially marry hinders monogamy.

Peruse the gay relationships section of a bookstore, and you will find that authors of the most popular titles are not only aware of the challenge of monogamy, but also have opinions (often very strong opinions) as to why such a challenge exists. Almost all agree, however, that unresolved psychological issues are the root cause. In just the past three years, as examples, we've been informed that our monogamy challenges are the result of often less than nurturing relationships with parents (the renowned Richard Isay in *Commitment and Healing)*, fear of intimacy (Martin Kantor in *Together Forever: The Gay Man's Guide to Lifelong Love*), and internalized homophobia (Jeffrey Chernin in *Get Closer: A Gay Men's Guide to Intimacy and Relationships*).

So why are gay men challenged by monogamy? Does it stem from internalized homophobia? A natural propensity for promiscuity? The effect of parental neglect? Low self-esteem? The availability of too many locations for sex? Maybe all of the above and even more? *And of even more importance, if we did work on these issues, would we be more successful with monogamy?* Based on streams of research that are typically unknown to the gay man on the street and ignored by writers of relationships books, the answer to this particular question is a resounding "no." Each of the above concerns likely holds true for some men, but the great strides that have been made in our understanding of human sexuality in the fields of psychology, sexology, and brain research illuminate just how inescapably challenging monogamy is for the majority of gay men. Many readers may be displeased with the research conclusions, but these fields do a far better job of elucidating gay male non-monogamy in comparison to even the best current existing explanations. The time is right to examine the research, to dispel conjecture and myth, and to begin a serious dialogue about monogamy in our community. After all, almost all of us will experience a monogamy-related concern at some point in our lives.

CHAPTER 1

The Gay Male Perspective

THEORIES ABOUND as to why gay men are challenged by monogamy. It's only fitting though that we begin our exploration of monogamy by asking gay men themselves why they think long-term monogamy is difficult.

Promiscuity

Ask a gay man about promiscuity and you will probably hear one of three responses, the first being that gay men are inveterately promiscuous. Consider some historic examples. The early years of the AIDS crisis resulted in an untold number of media reports on the sexual profligacy of gay men. According to Dr. June Osborn, a researcher at the federal National Institutes of Health (NIH): "Every time we do an NIH site visit, the definition of 'multiple sex partners' has changed. First it was twenty partners a year. That was 1975. Then in 1976, it was fifty partners a year. By 1978, we were talking about a hundred sexual partners a year, and now we're using the term to describe five hundred partners in a single year" (as cited in Rotello, 1997).

Even now, the media is saturated with reports on methamphetamine and gay men and how this drug can turn even the most reticent gay male into an uncontrollable sex fiend. Concurrently, sexually transmitted diseases in the gay community are on the rise again, even those thought conquered, such as syphilis. A recent review of data from New York City found that 80 percent of respondents had visited a sex-specific venue for the sole purpose of having often-anonymous sexual activity and reported a median of six different partners over the six months prior to the study interview (Peterman, et al. 2005).

Of course, many gay men refuse to pejoratively label the gay male community as promiscuous, and they refer us to studies ranging from the late 1970s to the present indicating that 40 percent to 60 percent of gay men report they are in a steady relationship and that some of these couples have been together more than twenty years. Such findings, while seeming to bode well for gay men and monogamy, really tell us nothing about actual sexual behaviors. After all, a male couple that has been together twenty years could still have experienced innumerable flings or "affairettes" (a noun I first encountered in Martin Kantor's *Together Forever: A Gay Man's Guide to Lifelong Love* (2005) and which I have become fond of). Recall the scenario of Ed and John that introduced this book.

According to the Kinsey Institute, heterosexual males ages 30 to 44 report an average of six to eight female sexual partners in their lifetime. Females of the same age group report four sexual partners in their lifetime. In contrast, the 2006 annual *Advocate* sex poll found that almost 50 percent of gay male respondents reported having *at least* twenty-one sex partners in their lifetime, and 23 percent reported more than a hundred partners. Earlier polls found that approximately 30 percent of gay male respondents reported two to five partners over the previous twelve months, and almost 20 percent reported six to twenty in the same time period. Many gay men double or triple in one year the number of sexual partners that a heterosexual male would like to have *in a lifetime,* which, according to a 1993 study that asked heterosexual males to estimate the number of sexual partners they would ideally have over their lifetime, is, on average, eighteen (Buss & Schmitt 1993).

If readers are anything like me, they can relate not only their own personal anecdotes of a "spouse" who cheated, but also examples from the lives of their gay friends. One of the doctors I interviewed for this book—a gentleman whose primary population consists of urban gay males—said candidly: "All gay men are whores." (I believe that this was the comment of a man still hurting from a failed relationship he *thought* was monogamous.) All gay men are not whores, but there is sufficient aggregate and anecdotal evidence to suggest that promiscuity plays a central part in the lives of many gay men.

There is sparse research on how the ready availability of other men for sex influences monogamy in committed relationships. We do know that heterosexual males exposed to images of attractive women report a decreased level of commitment to their current relationship partner. David Buss, a recognized pioneer in the study of the evolution of human sexuality, points out that our distant ancestors, living in small groups of 50 to 200 individuals, may have had less than two dozen potential mates to choose. In contrast, especially for those living in urban environments, we come in contact with thousands of possible mates. "[We] are bombarded by media images of attractive models on a scale that has no historical precedent and that may lead to unreasonable expectations about the quality and quantity of available mates" (Buss 2000, p. 16). We might speculate, then, that the actual availability of sex partners, rather than mere media images as presented to straight males in these studies, might have more than just a marginal effect on commitment for male couples. As further evidence, Donald Symons, the University of California professor of anthropology who first introduced the concept of hard-wired sexual similarities between gay and straight males, finds that the "unprecedented opportunity" of willing gay men to engage in sexual activity is one of the most pressing factors affecting gay monogamy (1979, p. 297).

Opportunity

Until two years ago in Philadelphia, my hometown, there existed a small parcel of semi-wooded land bordered on one edge by the Schuylkill River and on the other by a major traffic artery entering the city. Once, while on a long bike ride in my early twenties, I stopped there to sit on the grass and have a sports drink—and learned that I had inadvertently set myself up as willing and available for sex. Resembling a scene from a gay version of *Night of the Living Dead,* men of all shapes and colors suddenly materialized in the shadows of the trees. Some just stood there immobile and watched me. Others began to fondle their genital regions, and two of the most daring actually pulled out their penises for my perusal. I have to be honest that I was transfixed, although I did not participate in any post-exercise sexual activity. When I later told friends about my experience, I was informed that this was "Gay Acres," the most popular gay pick-up spot in the city.

In addition to the availability of other gay men for sex, the availability of venues conducive to gay sex can be another roadblock on the path to monogamy. Studies often cite the array of gay meeting places, particularly clubs and bars, as a major factor for the sexual profligacy of its subjects. This was also a key feature during the height of the AIDS epidemic, when cities began to close long-existing bathhouses, which were perceived as vectors for the spread of the disease. The availability of sexual venues—places for quick oral sex or mutual masturbation with a willing if unknown stranger—is certainly not new information to the majority of gay men. Consider two of the most popular titles in the gay travel publishing market: The *Damron* and *Spartacus* travel guides. Not only are readers informed of gay clubs and restaurants, but also of adult male movie theaters, steam rooms, sex clubs, "massage parlors," and escort services.

Not all gay couples espouse a desire for monogamy, but for those who do believe that monogamy is a core component of a committed relationship, relationship experts say that there are proactive and preventative measures men supposedly can take to reduce sexual mishaps, including avoiding environments associated with gay sex. One popular writer on the subject even suggests that committed male couples living in urban environments (particularly "gay ghettos") move to less sex-hospitable rural sections of their state. Actually, we are told, the less contact we have with other gay men, the less chance there will be for extra-relationship sexual contact.

The avoidance of environments and associated triggers that cue unwanted behaviors is certainly not a new concept and has been a recommended intervention for many self-control problems, including gambling, overeating, drug use, and, yes, sex.

From the therapeutic perspective, one of the primary therapeutic interventions for men with sexual control disorders is the removal of stimuli associated with problematic sexual behaviors. If, then, every bathhouse and gay bookstore were suddenly closed down, would impromptu gay sex suddenly stop and rates of monogamy rise?

The argument for closing venues associated with male same-sex sexual activity has both adherents and critics, and such an experiment took place in San Francisco during the tremulous early years of the AIDS crisis. Those supportive of closing these locations iterate their belief that such a measure decreases the amount of unsafe sex and thus HIV and other sexual disease transmission. Those who oppose enforced closures claim that it drives unsafe sexual behavior underground, where little education and testing are possible. As it stands, there is no conclusive evidence that closing these venues has decreased the amount of sexual contact and the spread of HIV. The reality is that if we closed every current venue known to be conducive to gay sex, others would arise to take their place.

In a recent interview with the National Parks and Recreation Society, I was informed that the primary "sexual nuisance" in state and national parks is the use of these often-secluded areas for gay male solicitation and outright sexual activity. By far the biggest complaint is the use of public bathrooms in these facilities for such activities. In fact, the primary source of consistent damage to these bathrooms is vandalism, most specifically graffiti denoting times and availabilities for male liaisons and the drilling of glory holes between stalls. Some state parks officials decided that the most effective method of eradicating this public nuisance was simply to raze entire bathroom facilities and, in their place, install portable toilets. Park staff noted that the amount of sexual activity occurring near the bathrooms was immediately curtailed, but the overall amount of gay male sexual activity in the parks did not decrease. Men instead found different places to meet up in the same parks.

As a therapist working with gay men, I have been astounded by some of the environments that can be briefly amenable to sexual activity. And my work with gay youth has led me to appreciate even more the underlying human creativity that is brought to bear in finding locations for sexual flings, as young people don't have access to the venues open to gay adults. Gay males will, without doubt, find places to meet and have sex no matter what obstacles are placed in their way.

The ability to hook up online for sex may reduce the numbers of men who visit bathhouses, public bathrooms, and other park settings. In fact, we are just now beginning to explore the effect of the Internet on the sexual activities of gay men. In my own work and that of my colleagues, we indeed have anecdotal evidence that some men have stopped visiting these areas now that they can arrange a meeting for sex in the privacy of their own homes, thus avoiding recognized safety threats and the specter of legal prosecution associated with public sexual activity. This does not mean, though, that the amount of gay male sexual activity has decreased; only that it has moved into more private locations.

For couples determined to remain monogamous, moving out of the gay ghetto and terminating Internet service may indeed reduce temptations. But for how long? Temptations often arise internally, in our fantasies and daydreams, and the real opponent in our attempts at monogamy is ourselves.

The Promises of Marriage

In December 2005, Sir Elton John "married" David Furnish under a new law in the United Kingdom that recognized civil partnerships and granted the same rights conferred on married heterosexual couples. The myriad press reports of the ceremony repeatedly say that the couple exchanged "vows." Most people would contend that a wedding vow incorporates some aspect of sexual fidelity. I admit, then, that I was surprised to learn that many secular wedding vows do not necessarily overtly mention monogamy or sexual fidelity, even if it is still implied. Religious wedding vows, in contrast, almost always demand faithfulness and fidelity.

This brings us to the third and final of the triad of obstacles that are thought to plague gay men determined to be monogamous. We are told that legal recognition of gay unions on par with heterosexual unions would promote a more monogamy-friendly environment (or at least make adultery too costly to contemplate). A gay man might think twice before engaging in an adulterous affair that just might lead to divorce court and possible financial penalties. But is this true?

Few couples in history have received such public scrutiny as Prince Charles and Princess Diana. Married on July 29, 1981, the couple exchanged vows in front of 3,500 invited congregants and a global television audience of 750 million. And if weddings vows were not in themselves sufficient enough reason to remain faithful, the public expectations foisted upon this fairytale couple by millions of people added additional incentive. But soon after their separation, the public was to learn that, in spite of their public vows, both partners had been unfaithful during the course of their marriage. Vows and a public ceremony do not necessarily result in monogamy, a fact that many disappointed spouses learn every year.

Sanctioned gay unions do offer benefits. The American Psychological Association position on gay marriages found that married men and women have higher levels of health and well-being than cohabiting but unmarried couples (Herek 2006). Public recognition of a union increases each partner's sense of security in the relationship, offers more social support, and grants privileged financial and legal rights. In sum, publicly sanctioned unions offer a trove of tangible and intangible buffers against the unavoidable travails of life. Of no less importance, a formal commitment is a deterrent to relationship dissolution and increases the likelihood that two men will not simply end their relationship when conflict inevitably arises. However, it is naïve to believe that an exchange of vows can somehow constrain our behavior throughout all the vicissitudes and opportunities of life. As evidence, one of the most common issues that propel a male couple into counseling centers on "opening the relationship" to other sexual partners. Instead of simply terminating their relationship, males who have made a commitment to each other now enter therapy to assist in their decision making about monogamy. A formal commitment does not prevent a desire for additional sexual partners, but it is likelier to drive a committed couple into counseling to discuss the option.

A vow made during a state of infatuation will hold far less firmly six years later, when sexual satisfaction in the relationship is on the wane and that new male secretary is coming across as quite available. Promises and verbal commitments to sexual fidelity often come to naught when hardwired sexual desire is activated. Statistics on infidelity in heterosexual couples offers no support for the belief that formal commitment cements long-term monogamy. Actually, instead of securing monogamy, it is the dynamics of the relationship itself that may motivate a partner (or both partners) to additional sexual trysts, as we shall see.

Finally, it's important to remember that not every gay couple even desires marriage at all. Many find the notion of a formalized commitment quite objectionable. Some believe that a formal commitment service—whether offered through a civil institution or a church—adds nothing of value to a couple. Since this is not a book on gay politics, we won't address this topic any further. However, it should be clear that a great many gay males would refrain from a formal commitment even if one were sanctioned.

SO WHAT ARE WE LEFT WITH at this point in our examination? The most salient point is that the three causal factors purported to undermine even the most sincere efforts at monogamy in male couples have varying levels of legitimacy. In ascending order of influence, society's refusal to acknowledge gay unions probably has a marginal effect on monogamous behaviors for gay men. Second, the abundance of gay venues does make sexual trysts easier but is certainly not the cause of monogamy failures. These venues arose specifically to meet the pre-existing demands of gay men. Finally, and the one I believe most important, there is promiscuity.

But is the common conceptualization of promiscuity an accurate description of gay male sexual activity? Or is there a more accurate definition—one that recognizes and takes into account the underlying physiological hardwired reasons for the often astoundingly high rates of sexual activity in the gay community? To begin answering those questions, we must first see what therapists say about monogamy and gay men.

CHAPTER 2
Therapists Speak

DWAYNE AND TERRENCE waited a year before deciding to live together; they wanted to be certain that they really knew each other before making a commitment. Terry owned his home, and Dwayne, who was renting an apartment, terminated his lease to move in with him. It was after the big move that their problem started. Dwayne stopped wanting sex. It wasn't a gradual occurrence; it happened suddenly and, at least from the perspective of Terry, inexplicably. Cuddling, kissing, and other forms of affection were evident, but Dwayne would not even offer to masturbate Terry. Any type of genital involvement was inscrutably off limits.

Terry, being a thoughtful and not particularly outspoken man, resigned himself to the sexual predicament. He certainly wasn't happy, but from his perspective, there was more to a relationship than sex. He compensated for the lack of carnality by increasing his own masturbation while viewing online pornography. When, one morning, Dwayne accidentally walked in on Terry in one of these self-pleasuring sessions, Dwayne realized that he needed to take some action. After a week of reflection, he offered a rather magnanimous suggestion: Terry would be allowed to engage in sexual activity with other men. It was at this juncture that they decided to seek the input of a professional therapist.

When men in a couple decide to investigate issues of monogamy, they often seek the input of others, including friends, confidants, and professional therapists and counselors who work with gay couples. And most often there is an underlying assumption that something is amiss in the relationship. Possibly one partner is dealing with issues that affect both men in the couple, or maybe the dynamics of the couple itself are to blame. But it is almost always taken for granted that something must be wrong within that couple. The next several pages will introduce a veritable catalogue of the most noted developmental and relationship issues for gay men that are known to have a pernicious influence on male couples.

If, upon perusing the information in this chapter, readers find that these issues really don't apply to them or their relationships, they may indeed be right. We will contemplate the consideration that nonmonogamy may not be the result of unresolved individual and couples' issues.

Therapists Takes Sides on Monogamy

Pick up any book on gay male relationships and you will without doubt find a section on monogamy. It may be nothing more than a paragraph, while, at the other extreme, it may take several chapters to contain the topic. If a reader were inclined to categorize the opinions of therapists and counselors regarding gay men and monogamy, he would find that there are three distinct camps. The first promotes monogamy and only monogamy as the ideal for gay couples, and some therapists and authors are exceedingly strident in this recommendation. For this first group, nonmonogamy is unworkable in the long run, though its tantalizing short-term benefits are certainly appealing. However, the risk of disease transmission, jealousy, and questions of underlying trust are bound to sink the relationship. The second group consists of those apparently still sitting on the fence and unwilling to take a firm stance one way or the other. The professionals in this second group believe that it would be better if we were monogamous, but since so many gay men are not, we might as well learn how to work with this lifestyle; for this camp, nonmonogamy is expected and even acceptable, but it is still secondary to monogamous relationships. The third and final camp endorses nonmonogamy as a realistic and workable alternative to monogamy, and some of its adherents quietly support nonmonogamy while others are as outspoken as their monogamy-only colleagues are in their beliefs.

The first two camps agree that nonmonogamous interest is often an outcome of underlying and unresolved personal and relationship issues. They also contend that if gay men would work on these issues and any other concerns that have stymied their own personal development, their relationships would improve, and, in the end, interest in nonmonogamy would disappear or, at least, be markedly reduced. In other words, an improved relationship decreases interest in seeking sexual pleasures outside of the relationship.

Internalized homophobia, gender-role conflict, lack of support, and delayed adolescence are considered the most prevalent obstacles that derail gay male relationships and, as a result, monogamy.

Internalized Homophobia

A gay male that has internalized negative messages about homosexuality tends to believe on some level that he is somehow inadequate or damaged. He has often developed shame about his identity and learned not to trust other people, and he maintains an emotional distance in relationships. Obviously these are not ideal characteristics for a healthy long-term relationship.

Admittedly it is impossible for gay males to completely escape the pernicious societal influences that lead to homophobia, and likely homophobia is present in all gay men. The amount present, however, can have extremely deleterious effects. First, it's difficult for another person to love us if we don't love ourselves (unless of course we find another gay man who is equally internally homophobic, which really sets up some powerfully pernicious relationship dynamics). If a gay man experiences shame about his identity, it is likely that he will not be comfortable exhibiting physical contact in public places and that he will have difficulty with intimacy, and the issue of trust will surface repeatedly.

In the example of Terry and Dwayne that opened this chapter, the therapist discovered that Dwayne had become infamous in his fundamentalist church after it was learned that he was living with another man. This occurred at the time that the topic of "men on the down low" was making headlines. Dwayne had been able to hide his sexual preference as long as he had maintained a single lifestyle, but now that he was living with another man, the rumor and innuendo that had quietly surrounded him surfaced in his congregation. Though Dwayne lied and told his congregation that Terry was a cousin and that their cohabitation was a means of saving money, the pressure from his church and the doubt and internalized homophobia he had maintained for almost his entire adult life combined to make sexual contact with Terry an impossibility.

Gender-Role Conflict

After internalized homophobia, the second most common issue for gay couples from the therapeutic standpoint is male gender stereotypes. Such roles have been found to be harmful in heterosexual relationships, but for straight males who are brought up to devalue vulnerability and to be autonomous, self-reliant, powerful, aggressive, and competitive, they are at least in theory complimented by females who are just as often raised to demonstrate opposing gendered behaviors. Complimentary roles can often still clash, of course—but if two partners share the same gender roles, we often encounter an outright internecine war.

Little boys are taught to compete, to hide any sign of weakness (particularly emotions such as fear and sadness), and not to display affection. Additionally, males learn to undervalue empathy skills and are not taught how to take the perspective of another person. We bring these characteristics into our adult relationships. In a relationship of two men, where both have been taught to deride emotional displays (other than anger) and where disagreements immediately evoke a battle in which partners fight to prove their superiority, control issues constitute a veritable third person in the relationship. Another recurrent problem is anger; it can be very difficult to reconcile arguments if neither male is willing to put down the defenses and simply listen. Indeed, many gay men rely on sex as the balm for disagreements, avoiding the often-unpleasant task of actual dialogue and instead allowing physicality to stand in the place of the hard work of meaningful disclosure.

Finally, gender expectations straitjacket gay men with regard to their own freedom of expression. If a man acts less masculine or is emotionally expressive, his partner may castigate and deride him for this unseemly feminine behavior. Gay men can and do shackle themselves even more tightly into the constraints of gender expectations, so that vulnerability and the intimacy that blossoms from it are quashed.

In sum, many males do not know how to seek emotional support and nurturance from another male or how to give it when a partner is in need of just such consideration.

Lack of Support

The third in the quartet of the most problematic relationship issues from a therapeutic standpoint is the lack of social support for gay relationships. Recall from the first chapter that a recent American Psychological Association study on gay relationships found that they offer substantial benefits. A lack of legal sanction has thus far prevented many gay men from being recipients of benefits that are taken for granted by established heterosexual couples, particularly tax breaks, insurance benefits, and control of medical decisions in catastrophic incidents.

Societal disapproval of gay relationships also has pernicious drawbacks that one might not immediately consider in comparison to the high-profile challenges just mentioned. At the top of the list is the presence of family members who are less than enthusiastic or even outright hostile about acknowledging a son's sexuality, and, to add insult to injury, his male partner. Gay men who have been together for years may have to hide their relationship in order not to disturb a family member. Additionally, straight couples tend to have an extended family they can turn to when problems arise, but this cannot be assumed for a male couple. Many people turn to their families when a relationship begins to go astray, but if a family is not accepting of a gay relationship or is simply uncomfortable with the concept of two men in a loving relationship, a troubled man lacks access to this source of family succor. It's unfortunately not a rarity that gay men must make a choice between family and partner; whichever is chosen, the emotional fallout from the choice is destined to haunt a man, often for a lifetime. The lack of family support is also one of the primary reasons gay men are noted for creating a substitute family comprised of close friends.

A lack of support for gay relationships occurs at more than the level of the family. In the not-too-distant past, it was assumed that the only way a gay male could achieve a stable identity was to come "out of the closet" and acknowledge himself as homosexual to family, friends, coworkers, and just about anybody who had a meaningful role in his life. Gay, proud, and outspoken was the mantra, and for many, such a stance is indeed helpful, but in a world that continues to discriminate against sexual minorities, sometimes it is not beneficial and may even be harmful. A male could very well experience, for example, subtle and overt unwanted consequences in his career that far outweigh the benefits that come from a public acknowledgement of homosexuality. As these consequences become recognized, therapists no longer push gay men to come out to the world (or at least their small portion of it) until they are ready. But even though therapists know that the coming-out process must be made at the personal level, with a careful examination that weighs the pros and cons of such an important decision, a gay male might not demonstrate the same understanding and patience with his partner.

When one partner is open about his sexuality and the other is not, relationship issues arise. One partner may feel resentment that he cannot have a more out lifestyle, while the other may feel pressured to reveal aspects of his life that he would prefer remain private. Arguments may arise as to who the couple should be out to. In the end, both partners tend to become judgmental about each other's decisions.

Delayed Adolescence

The majority of straight men and women partake of dating during their adolescence, and many of these experiences lead to some form of sexual involvement. Thus they have likely learned at least the rudiments of the basic give and take required in a relationship. We cannot take this for granted when it comes to gay men: gay adolescents have far fewer opportunities for dating, simply because we are a minority and not surrounded with obvious and viable dating partners. In addition, the shame felt by many a gay male adolescent prevents him from opening up to others who might have an interest. As a result, we cannot assume that other gay men have learned simple relational skills inculcated into straight males during their adolescence. I, for example, work with men who haven't mastered some basics, including not talking too much about oneself on a first date, not being too aggressive about setting a second date, and not discussing past boyfriends, particularly in negative terms.

Because so many gay men did not have the opportunity to experiment with dating in their teenage years, many experience a delayed adolescence in which they begin to explore the relational and sexual aspects of life in their twenties and thirties. Gay males are so flushed with excitement with their freedom to express sexual urges and longings that were thoroughly concealed in their younger years that the thought of settling down in a serious relationship appears almost anticlimactic. There are too many men and there is too much sex to have before they are willing to consider long-term monogamy. We all know that it is hard to commit when we are distracted by other potential lovers, and in the delayed adolescent stage experienced by gay men, such distractions abound.

Additional Concerns

In addition to the four therapeutic concerns for gay males presented above, professionals commonly cite several other issues they believe have a negative effect on long-term monogamy.

A Lack of Role Models

In many cultures, elders are revered, but this is certainly not true in the United States. Looking one's age is to be avoided as long as possible, and regardless of sexual orientation, people don't want to look "old" or aged. This is compounded in the gay male community. At least in the straight world, older folks, though incorrectly perceived as nonsexual beings, are often accorded some stature for life experience and acquired wisdom. In the gay world, older gay men are not only seen as non-sexual but are not even sought out for their knowledge and acumen. Indeed, a recurrent fear I hear from many gay men is that they will end up like "Ted" (or one of hundreds of other names), the "old guy" who sits alone in the bar on the weekend looking for some young jock to take home for the night, even if it means having to pay for him.

Many children grow up with the active presence of grandparents, and they offer a role model, enabling their grandchildren to see that one possible path in life is to take a spouse and contentedly grow old together. How many older male couples, though, can act as role models for the younger generations? Older gay men tend to associate with others of the same age range, since younger males often avoid them at all costs or maintain a superficial politeness in their attempts to get away from an encounter as quickly as possible. They are unwelcome or persona non grata in their own worlds. Avoidance negates opportunities for the young to learn from the old; older male couples who may have been in relationships for decades can therefore not stand as role models for younger generations. In effect, young gay men do not have a mental template for long-term relationships and the ability to stay together through the travails and vicissitudes of life, simply because those who manage this feat remain hidden from view.

Brief Courtship

It never ceases to amaze me that so many gay men jump right

through the courtship stage and begin a serious relationship—often moving in together—after only several months. And since they are in a state of infatuation, a topic that we will explore in Chapter Four, attempts to sway them from this ill-fated decision cannot be heard amid the cacophony of passion. The expert on gay relationships Betty Berzon wrote that if she had her way, gay couples would have to wait at least six months before they move in together. During this time, they would have to actually get to know each other as whole people rather than just as sexual beings.

Coming to know another person is a process that takes years, even decades. And even then there will always be secrets that we remain oblivious to. We cannot truly know another person in a few short months, particularly when both partners are trying to make the very best impression on each other. However, many gay men don't know this, because they had limited dating experience in adolescence or simply don't care while in the throes of passion. But after a year, the real challenges of the relationship begin, and many will find that they are cohabiting with another male with whom they are incompatible, or, worse, don't even like.

The Easy Termination of Gay Relationships

It will be the rare married or coupled heterosexual male that does not experience sexual temptation for a third person from outside the relationship. Many will not pursue this temptation simply because of the consequences, and the more consequences that could occur, the more likely one is to seriously consider his actions. But what are the consequences for a gay male if he sexually goes astray or if he wants to trade in his current partner for a different or younger model? In comparison to heterosexual marriages, the consequences are far fewer, and relationship therapists speculate that this is another negative influence on long-term relationships.

One of the positive effects of a publicly recognized and socially sanctioned union is that it is a deterrent to simply ending a relationship when problems arise; it is more difficult for one or both partners to simply walk away without any lasting consequence. And as we saw in Chapter One, this is a reason gay men give in support of gay marriage. Indeed, many gay men expect a quick and comparatively painless dissolution to their relationship when challenges surface, and such an outcome is more probable when there is limited support by family members who would rather pretend the relationship didn't exist in the first place and when there are no children to consider.

Some therapists bemoan the fact that there is now an expectation in the gay community that the process of relationship termination should be hassle free. Gay men often do not enter relationships with a realistic appraisal of what they entail, and many are simply not prepared for the hard work that comes with the process. The ability to easily end a relationship reduces the chance that two men will hang in there and work out problems.

Gay Culture

It is certainly not an overstatement to say that gay culture is antipathetic to long-term gay male relationships. Gay culture emphasizes beauty, youth, and the freedom to act on one's sexual desires. Indeed, from the gay male perspective, a relationship counts as "long-term" if it has lasted all of two years. Living within such an environment certainly is not helpful for commitment or monogamy, and therapists often help couples disengage themselves from the typical gay scene and instead associate with other couples in environments that do not promote unbridled sexual freedom.

Expectations

As homosexuality has been seen as an aberration throughout much of history, gay men have to cope with the widespread belief that their relationships are seen not only as shams but also as unworkable in the long run. Such a history understandably leads to an expectation that a relationship between gay males cannot work. Indeed, many men exploit the relationship for all the pleasures it can offer and, when it begins to show signs of wear, move on to another man. A long-term relationship built upon the expectation that it cannot last will, obviously, have inherent difficulties from the start.

The Minority Perspective

A 1998 study asked participants to write narratives concerning their personal experiences with affairs. One of the themes that emerged was a belief that if one married the right person, there would be no temptation for infidelity. Indeed, many gay men and the therapists that work with them would concur. But what if this isn't true? What if we did indeed find a partner that suits us wonderfully but are still drawn by the temptation of sexual contact outside the relationship? More and more therapists are recognizing that nonmonogamy cannot be resolved via even the best therapeutic interventions. They are still a minority, but their ranks are growing.

Could you imagine a therapist suggesting an exploration of additional sexual partners for heterosexual and lesbian couples? Sexual infidelity is a cause for divorce, separation, or at the least, a serious reexamination of the relationship for such couples, yet an increasing number of therapists who work with male couples challenge the reigning hegemony of monogamy. Greenan and Tunnell explicitly say the same thing in their well-regarded 2003 clinical text, *Couple Therapy with Gay Men,* in which they recognize that nonmonogamy would be a serious problem for all other couples but needs to be approached as nonpathological for male couples. It is only with gay men that we would even begin to contemplate the interpersonal advantages of extra-relational sexual partners.

No one denies that male relationships experience the very same problems that all couples encounter and that this is further compounded by issues salient to only gay couples. Professionals are also in agreement that by working on areas such as internalized homophobia, gender-role conflicts, and the augmentation of a support system, relationships will be improved and both partners will find more satisfaction. It is at this point, though, where differences between the opposing camps discussed earlier surface. Many believe that relationship improvement and resulting satisfaction will naturally lead to less interest in perusing sexual activity outside of that relationship. As we will see, this is not necessarily true.

To illustrate this, consider the difference in responses by

male and female college students to the question "What would be your motives for having sexual intercourse?" The majority of female responses centered on demonstrations of love and commitment. In contrast, the majority of male responses did not even mention love or commitment. Instead they gave evidence of the instrumentality that men place on sex (Shibley Hyde 1996):

- *I need it.*
- *To gratify myself.*
- *I'm tired of masturbation.*

When it comes to men and infidelity, the research tells us that male desire for sexual novelty, experimentation, and excitement are just as predictive of sexual liaisons outside a relationship as issues occurring within that relationship. Working on one's internal "baggage" and/or issues disturbing to a couple can only help a relationship; yet it does not ensure monogamy, or even a reduction of sexual interest in other partners.

CHAPTER 3

Monogamous or Not?

ALL KNOWN SOCIETIES have incorporated a variation of marriage as an institution, and it is not surprising that so many gay men have accepted the romanticized image of one pair residing in perpetual conjugal bliss though all the travails of life. So many pine, sometimes silently and sometimes to all that will listen, for a long-term committed relationship. However, with divorce rates as high as they are for heterosexual marriages, is it possible that we have chosen the wrong model to emulate? In spite of the fact that we have a growing availability of professional resources perched and ready to analyze and intervene in gay relationships, many gay men remain unsuccessful in achieving their desired long-term monogamous relationship in spite of their best efforts. So we keep going back, seeking more advice on how to achieve at least a semblance of an ideal relationship, believing that some therapist, some book, some source of inspiration must have the right answer. But if our ideal is unobtainable, we can spend our lives trying to obtain a relationship pattern that will never occur. What if it never even existed?

It makes perfect sense that gay men have accepted the ideal

of a monogamous relationship. But the ideal of monogamy remains just that: an ideal. In reality, monogamy is far less obtainable than we have been brought up to believe and, additionally, far less common than we have been taught.

The Polar Extremes of Relationships

If we group expectations about relationships along a continuum, we find the two polar extremes informative for our examination of monogamy. On one end, we have a vision of sexual relationships that is best depicted in the utopian musings of the eighteenth-century French philosopher Jean-Jacques Rousseau. He believed that humans were originally free of the concept of property and ownership until society corrupted that idyllic existence. The absence of ownership, he posited, even applied to sexual relationships; no person could "own" another, and humans were free to delight in sexual experiences with whomever they wished without the intrusion of jealousy and suspicion.

At the other end of the continuum, we have an understanding of relationships that started with Plato. He wrote that in the beginning all humans, called Androgynes, were self-composed units with four arms and legs, two heads, and double genitals—two fused individuals, creatures completely contented and fulfilled. However, the gods were angered by their smugness and forcibly severed them into two separate beings. It was then the fate of each human to spend his or her life seeking out that one other person who was his or her other half, the perfect match who would make both persons whole. A relationship with just any other individual would not work.

Both these extremes exist in the gay male world. There are gay men who move on from one sexual adventure to another, and there are others who believe that they have found their perfect lover or who are still out there seeking him. But most people do not live at the extremes and, it is safe to say, most gay men fall somewhere between the two poles of Plato and Rousseau. A gay man in that vast middle ground will want a good romantic match with one person, while still desiring uncommitted and satisfying sexual encounters with other men.

Both Plato and Rousseau were wrong about the sexual origins of man, but their influence can still be found in the expectations gay men have about relationships.

The Rarity of Monogamy

Expectations about relationships and monogamy play no small role in the gay male experience, and those expectations often lie at the polar extremes described above. For example, we would find Martin Kantor, the author of *Together Forever: The Gay Man's Guide to Lifelong Love,* at the Platonic end: he informs us that "monogamy is the greatest gift you will ever have to give to each other."

Holding to an ideal, however, can put us in an untenable and ultimately hopeless position. As a therapist, one of the most common complaints and concerns I hear from clients is that they are unhappy and unsatisfied with their lives. Many people enter therapy with an image of their idealized life, and the difference between the ideal and the actual is a source of emotional pain. The chasm between an ideal of monogamy and the shifting sexual desires in our daily life can also be a source of frustration and discontent at both the individual and couples' levels.

When I let people know that I was writing a book on gay men and monogamy, I had no challenge finding men who were willing to share their experiences. My discussions uncovered a widespread, overriding belief that monogamy is the ultimate tier in a hierarchy of relationships, the idealized relationship goal for gay men. And while many questioned whether they would reach this goal, all too few actually questioned the goal of monogamy itself.

Is it possible, then, that maybe, just maybe, gay men have trouble with monogamy not because of their personal weaknesses or the host of issues catalogued here earlier, but rather because the goal itself is unreachable and never really was? Are we striving for a relationship pattern that doesn't suit human beings (and maybe most other mammals as well)? Are we really sexually weak, or is the very goal of monogamy itself misguided?

Adhering to an ideal can blind us to reality. It can lead us to ignore contrary evidence and misinterpret the facts to fit pre-existing conclusions. Not too long ago, for example, the expectation was that most animals were monogamous, and exceptions to this were considered anomalous in the natural world. But scientists have since found that the reverse is now true: monogamous animals are now believed to be outside the general norm.

You didn't buy this book as a field guide to nature, and my guess is that you won't find many therapists or relationship books for gay men discussing the mating habits of the prairie vole. Regardless, animal studies do offer some fascinating input into a comprehensive understanding of monogamy that can shed some light on our own mating preferences; the study of birds in particular has highlighted the discrepancy between our perceptions of monogamy and the reality.

Most bird species appear to live a monogamous existence; a mating pair often nest together and copulate exclusively with each other. But modern DNA profiling negates this belief. Most birds *appear* to have monogamous relationships, but in actuality they are quite fond of sexual relationships with other birds beside their partners. Across many bird species, both males and females engage in these sexual encounters, and the chicks in the nest of papa bird have some likelihood of not actually being biologically related to him at all.

Many species appear to be monogamous in that they cohabit, share resources, have sex, and raise their young together—what is termed "social monogamy"—yet the birds of these species do not practice sexual exclusivity; they have "hidden" sex with other partners. Unsurprisingly, this same scenario plays out in the human realm, and of course among gay couples. There are many such couples in which one man (or both) is involved in clandestine sexual activity, even though as a couple they cohabit and share resources, including, sometimes, the raising of children.

One of the most telling interviews I conducted was with a therapist who spoke with great respect for the monogamous male couples he worked with, particularly those in relationships lasting more than a decade. "But how do you know they're actually monogamous, other than by their own report," I asked him. Did he furtively follow them in their day-to-day routines to monitor for sexual misadventures? Could these couples be like our feathered friends, simply appearing to be monogamous? Even birds are known to hide their sexual wanderings from their partners and create an elaborate panoply of behaviors both to unobtrusively slip away for a quick sexual escapade and, afterward, to hide evidence of the liaison.

The therapist in question seemed reluctant to entertain this line of questioning. Finally, he took off his glasses and looked ruefully at the floor. In spite of his hope that his couples were monogamous, he had a "gut instinct" that this simply wasn't true. His response told me more about him than it did his couples. Here was a therapist who subscribed to the ideal of monogamy, and he expected his clients to do the same.

Our present stance on idealized monogamy fosters two conclusions that are really different sides to the same coin. One is that monogamy is the best and most advanced relationship pattern. The second is that other existing forms of relationship patterns are somehow "unnatural" or, at least, deserve a lower rank on a relationship hierarchy. Lest the reader think that I will be advancing some quasi-1970s version of the joys of free love and open relationships, let me put your concerns to rest. Even those kinds of relationships are fraught with challenges and may be even more unfeasible than monogamy in the long term, as we shall see. In truth, both strict monogamy and its polar opposite, unencumbered and uncommitted sexual encounters, are unsatisfying for most people; men in particular—whether straight, gay, or bisexual—desire a combination of both.

Monogamy and Society

In addition to strict monogamy, a range of other lifestyle options have been found in human society, including:

- *Remaining single*
- *Serial monogamy—a series of successive monogamous relationships*
- *Communal living*
- *Swinging and/or group sex*
- *Group marriage*
- *Two or more simultaneous committed relationships*
- *Extramarital relationships*
- *Polygamy*

And just as strict monogamy—sexual activity between two designated partners only—is a rarity among mammals, we find that it has also been a minority relationship pattern in every human culture that ever existed. Indeed, the most common relationship pattern for humans is social monogamy, defined as having one identified sexual partner with whom one establishes a household while also engaging in additional covert sexual flings. Women are not off the hook in this description, they too engage in sexual affairs, though not to the same extent as males. If this is true, how then did the idealized image of strict monogamy take hold in our society so that it is now the expectation for relationships?

To the best of our knowledge, human beings are the only creatures to socially impose monogamy. While there are indeed other animals that remain monogamous—admittedly the minority—it is certainly not because they have tacitly agreed to it. Most often, other creatures that adhere to a monogamous lifestyle do so because environmental conditions offer no opportunities for anything but monogamy. Having more than one mate often requires double (or triple) the amount of work. Now a male animal must not only protect and possibly supply sustenance for one mate, he now has to complete the same work for two. All the while, he will have to fend off sexual approaches by other males for his own mates. This may work in environments rich with resources, but in terrains sparse with the necessities for survival or that contain a fair number of predators, maintaining two mates or even simply engaging in sex with additional females is too exhausting and dangerous.

Even though we cannot completely rule out the effect of environmental conditions on human monogamy, societal influence plays a far more pivotal role. A 2005 *Newsweek* story titled "The Secret Lives of Wives" noted an increase in rates of female infidelity stemming from societal changes. While history offers irrefutable evidence that women have always engaged in adultery, until recently, the discovery of their adulterous involvement would result in grave social consequences, particularly the loss of the financially supportive spouse. However, as women have become increasingly financially independent, they have less to fear if an adulterous liaison is discovered. Nowadays, social embarrassment might be an outcome, but penury is unlikely. In addition, women now have more opportunities for meeting prospective male (and often female) sexual partners in workplace settings. Finally, technology such as cell phones and e-mail make it far easier to hide activity that is meant to remain clandestine. In sum, as societal changes affect the standing and roles of women, there is now less shame necessarily associated with female adultery. Where a woman would have been scorned by society at large in the not-too-distant past, she is now more likely to receive the commiseration of her friends and, possibly, even be a source of envy.

In her cross-cultural examination of monogamy, Pamela Druckerman wrote, "It turns out that countries, regions, and even neighborhoods have their own sexual cultures, which influence whether people are monogamous or not" (2007, p. 60).

The History of Human Monogamy

There is no evidence that our distant ancestors practiced strict monogamy. Some researchers hold to the belief that these early humans lived in a state of promiscuity in which there were no constraints on the sexual involvements of either gender. Most, however, believe that our ancestors were polygamous, defined as one sex having more than one sexual partner of the opposite sex (almost always, it was the male that had multiple partners), that they practiced serial monogamy (defined as maintaining a monogamous relationship for several years before moving on to another new monogamous relationship), or that they were socially monogamous.

Studies from around the world find that when couples part, they do so most often during their fourth year together. Anthropology expert Helen Fisher believes that our ancestors only mated long enough to rear a single child safely through infancy, an approximate time span of four years, before moving on to another mate. Such a strategy, incidentally, would have been beneficial for genetic diversity and would have been passed down through the eons.

Unlike many other living things, human babies need a lot of care after their birth. For some species, a newborn is already up on its feet in a matter of minutes to hours; other species give birth to babies that are able to tend to some of their own needs fairly rapidly, at least in comparison to a human child. This is not so for humans, and a newborn child enters the world unequipped for survival, and at least until fairly recently, success-ful survival would have depended on the support of at least two individuals.

As discussed earlier, one reason monogamy developed, sci-entists believe, was the influence of environmental constraints. It took two parents to maximize a child's chance for survival, and in the brutish world of our ancestors, where fluctuations in food supplies, weather, predators (both animals and other hu-mans), and disease were a daily threat to human existence, a child's survival was hardly a certainty. These conditions favored monogamy in early humans, just as they do for other species that require extended care for their offspring. But note here that I am not saying strict monogamy. Just as we saw with birds, in socially monogamous animal species, the individuals within mating couples still disappear into the foliage for a few hidden brief minutes with another sexual partner. It is likely that this was the same for our human ancestors; early men and women would have combined efforts to support their young, but it seems probable that they also would have left the cave oc-casionally for relations with another individual.

The Monogamy Conundrum

One gay man interviewed for this book summed it up tidily: "I just want a man that I can share my life with who isn't going to be having sex with other men behind my back. Is that too much to ask for?"

Is it too much to ask for a long-term relationship that spans decades and that maintains strict sexual monogamy? Many professional therapists and the gay men who seek their services do not believe that this is too much to ask for, and in fact, we are often told that with sufficient motivation and effort, it is within our reach.

But strict monogamy with no allowances for additional sexual dalliances goes against everything we know about the actual sexual behavior of humans. If the opportunities for an occasional sexual dalliance outside of an established relationship were completely eliminated, would this in turn increase the satisfaction levels of the men in the partnership? How can we be satisfied if we have evolved to seek meaningful relationships with another person and yet, at the same time, be desirous of frequent sexual involvements with new partners? If a gay man seeks engagement exclusively in uncommitted sexual activity, he will eventually be unsatisfied with the outcome. Conversely, if he invests all of his libido in one committed relationship he will also eventually yearn for someone new, even if only anonymous sexual encounters. Whichever path he chooses, he will find pleasures and often sublime delights, but also inevitable misgivings and unfulfilled longings.

The ideal of monogamy is the first of two societal assumptions about relationships that we have to consider in order to make definitive decisions about gay men and monogamy. The second is passionate love. Are humans like Plato's Androgynes? Is it possible to find one person who will satisfy all our needs? Is there one person with whom we can fall passionately in love and keep that fire burning forever? Many people, gay men included, believe this is possible in spite of divorce statistics that indicate otherwise.

CHAPTER 4

The Rise and Fall of Sexual Desire

ARE GAY MEN and straight men really that different? Differences in sexual orientation obfuscate what all men have in common with regard to sexual desires, passions, behaviors, and problems. Gay men and straight men can become aroused when they don't want to be and—for many, a much more uncomfortable occurrence—cannot become aroused when they do really want to be. There is no quantitative difference between the number of gay and straight men who develop fetishes, have premature ejaculation issues, experience erection problems as they age, and are turned on by the sight of a striking young adult in a state of undress.

Both gay and straight men share a desire to fall in love, and both also hope for the permanence of passion in spite of overwhelming contradictory evidence. Passion is wonderful, but so too is it a problem. It fades so quickly. The passion that envelops the early stages of a relationship is for many the most powerfully intoxicating positive emotion they will feel in their lives. One of the young men I mentor professionally, a customarily staid and laconic individual with a very serious outlook on life, recently fell in love. He now enters my office singing

47

Celine Dion songs, calls his boyfriend at least once an hour, and is often in a state of dreamy reverie. Because my professional focus is human sexuality, I have the temerity to ask questions one wouldn't generally ask in polite dialogue. This gentleman informed me that not only do he and his new beau make love several times a night, he also masturbates to fantasies of his beau and finds himself with unwanted erections throughout the day. By his own report, he is the happiest he has ever been. Based on what we know about the physiological and chemical, operation of the human body, we would find actual, quantifiable changes in the functioning of his brain.

I'm jealous. I remember what it was like to be swept up by the same feelings my young friend is experiencing, and I remember *those* nights, and I remember the intoxicating certainty that I had found the one person who could complete me forever. Even then I knew that certainty was faulty and unworkable, but I was in love and I willed myself into ignorance. I guess I'm an Androgyne at heart. But fifteen years can, and without doubt does, diminish passion.

Sometimes passion can fade after a relatively short period of time. Ryan, a 30-year-old schoolteacher, also found his true love and invited him to move into his condo within six months. Now, Ryan is not only smart but also startlingly attractive, and he never had a shortage of partners either for casual sex or extended relationships. But after the first year of life together with the man of his dreams, he found that passion was already fading. And with a bevy of available lovers and sexual partners vying for his attention, Ryan finds his desire for a new man more than just a passing thought. As this book is being written, Ryan is struggling with the question of just what to do.

Next time you're at the supermarket, take a look at the magazines lining the aisles. There will be at least one trumpeting this or that technique on how to rekindle the passion that once was so natural and spontaneous for a couple. Most are written for a female audience, but it's no different for males. A passionate and sexually satisfying relationship is now a requirement for a couple; when one or the other ends, so too, generally, does the couple's time together. Unfortunately, the longer a relationship lasts, the more likely we are to find that extra effort is needed to evoke passion. Some people don't even try, and sexual relations fall off precipitously as passion dims.

Just about every relationship experiences a falloff in the amount of sexual activity, but for some, sex practically stops. Women, more than men, respond by trying to recreate this once all-consuming passion; men, in contrast, respond with increased masturbation, use of pornography, attempts to engage a spouse in some variation of swinging behavior (such as introducing another sexual partner into the relationship), and the occasional (or frequent) use of outside sex partners.

I have worked with enough males—gay and straight—in therapy sessions to recognize a common theme. Men love their partners, whether women or other men. They dote on them. They think the world of them. Most would even give up their own lives for their welfare. But in spite of all this love, they find it difficult to experience lust for this person. They may have once masturbated to thoughts of their lover, but now masturbation focuses on images in magazines, and increasingly, the Internet. For many if not most couples, passion and love are not mutually compatible. There are reasons for this, common to all males, though it plays out in its own way for gay male couples.

You're Getting to Be
a Habit with Me

We think we can manage our passions far better than we really can. We think we can prevent ourselves from becoming attracted to another person or even falling in love. And we also think we can prevent ourselves from falling out of love. On a purely cognitive level, we believe we can stop the bleeding out of passion from *our* relationship, even when we see all the relationships around us falling apart. Young people can be forgiven for their overestimation of their ability to manage their sexual and romantic feelings based on their limited life experience. But I have worked with adult males with plenty of life experience who hold to the same belief, even after a succession of relationships in which passion did not last. Even when they acknowledge the transitory nature of passion, they cannot help but be swept away when it resurges in their lives. Or they become cynical and, instead of enjoying the passion with a new-found lover, are already preparing for its end.

As with monogamy, we tend to have an idealized image of passion. But also like monogamy, this ideal does not hold up to scrutiny. Even as I write this, I can easily recall the things I felt when I was swept up by passion; some were positive, some were sexual, some were an emotional rollercoaster careening between elation and despair. And on a few, brief occasions, some ignited outright hatred. When a person experiences passion, man or woman, gay or straight, emotions can vacillate quickly and wildly. Sometimes the person we desire fills every waking moment of our life. Sometimes we recognize our obsessiveness but cannot stop ourselves; often we don't want to stop. We can't see the negative aspects of the other person, or, if we can, we minimize their importance. I, for example, am a vehement nonsmoker, but in a past state of passionate euphoria was more than willing to overlook the tobacco aroma that filled my apartment for days after my lover would leave. We are willing to endure so much in the early stages of love, when passion is at its peak.

Passionate love seems to bring all our senses to the surface, and everything is felt more keenly and sharply. The good is great, and the bad is unbearable. While enraptured with passion, we believe that a trivial relationship infraction necessitates a complete reconsideration of that relationship. A year or two later the same incident wouldn't faze us in the least. In passion, the slightest slight can be a most painful rupture of all our mutual dreams that can only be healed by conversation into the wee small hours of the morning and the post-argument sex that is destined to occur.

Perhaps more than anything else, passion has sexual components. First, we are in a state of either constant sexual arousal or are able to achieve that state in a matter of moments. We are "horny" most of the day and cannot get enough intimate contact with a partner. These are the days when we are willing to forgo all the work we customarily take home on the weekend to spend two days in sexual bliss. Second, we typically lose interest in sex with other men. This doesn't mean that a hot guy walking down the street is invisible to us or that we don't take a second glance as he confidently rambles past. But passion leads to exclusivity, a focus on our current lover. One man I worked with, Bryce, summed up this experience pretty well. As a fanatic admirer of porn, he was able to rattle off a complete litany of male porn stars, their roles, and their rank along a continuum of penis size. Bryce also used videos and Internet sites for a substantial amount of masturbatory release. But once he became passionately involved with Mark, he was not only able to curtail all of these sexual outlets (and save plenty of money in the process) but even told me that he would be able to restrain himself from touching even the hottest of hot porn stars if he found one alone, naked, and willing in the back room of the gay bookstore. Bryce was willingly committed to maintaining a sexually exclusive relationship with Mark; in fact, Mark is all he desired. But unsurprisingly, as the passion between them waned, his interest in pornography resurged. For the majority, passion equates with intense sexual passion for one person and only that person who has captured our thoughts, emotions, and sexual desire.

Medicine and the sciences are helping us to understand passion, a topic once restricted to the proprietary musings of poets and philosophers. Anthropologist Helen Fisher, for example, created a stir in 2004 when she released her study of the chemistry of love. Fisher hypothesized that dopamine, a neurochemical that produces focused attention, motivation, goal-directedness, stamina, and exhilaration, was the key hormone that comes into play during passion. Her study used an MRI to identify the chemical activity in the brains of individuals passionately in love and found that the ventral tegmental area (VTA), a central part of the brain governing pleasure and emotion, was extremely active; not surprisingly, the VTA is also the key area of the brain for dopamine production. "No wonder lovers talk all night or walk till dawn, write extravagant poetry and self-revealing e-mails, cross continents or oceans to hug for just a weekend, change jobs or lifestyles, even die for one another," Fisher writes in her 2004 book, *Why We Love: The Nature and Chemistry of Romantic Love.* "Drenched in chemicals that bestow focus, stamina, and vigor, and driven by the motivating engine of the brain, lovers succumb to a Herculean courting urge." Fisher's study indicates that passion and love are more than emotions; they are also fundamental drives that underlie mating. In short, our brains compel us to seek passionate relationships.

There doesn't seem to be anything particularly romantic about placing individuals into MRI and PET scanners to measure brain activity or taking blood samples to analyze the chemical substrates of passion, but it has certainly been an eye-opening experience. Some researchers have even had subjects masturbate to ejaculation to monitor brain changes during the act. While it is far too early to offer an unequivocal description of passion from a scientific standpoint, there is no doubt that our brains are the focal point for this emotion. Research finds that the areas of the brain activated by passion are also activated by drug use; though there are of course differences, it is striking that addictive drugs (like cocaine) influence brain functioning in a fashion similar to passion, and dopamine changes in the brain are associated with both passion and addiction.

"Falling in love is a measurable biological state, akin to a manic episode or a bout of temporary insanity," writes Frank Pittman, a psychiatrist and expert in the study of infidelity in a 2005 issue of the *Journal of Couple and Relationship Therapy*. "It is overwhelming, like a neurochemical tidal wave, disorienting lives in ways that were not anticipated and can not be understood. Whether people enter affairs blindly or calculatedly, the neurochemistry of 'being in love' is extraordinarily difficult to escape and produces an experience akin to withdrawal from an addictive drug." Does this mean that we can experience withdrawal symptoms if the object of our passion is removed from us for too long? I refer back to the young man introduced earlier in this chapter. He displayed the behaviors of an addict, though his particular habit is another person rather than an illicit substance. He needed to phone his lover several times a day as if he was in need of a fix, and when this person went away for a family vacation for two weeks, my poor friend fell into a state of torpor, as if his neurochemistry was crashing. It may be anticlimactic to learn that the fire kindling great loves is largely the result of underlying brain function, but that knowledge helps us better understand why passion inevitably subsides.

The Fading of Passion

What happens to make us shift from sneaking out of our job for a little afternoon delight with the object of our desire to the inability to maintain an erection when that same person is right there in bed next to us? There are several possibilities.

Hormonal Changes

Testosterone is recognized for spiking sexual desire and creating the physical sensation of horniness that we associate with sexual arousal, so it would seem natural that a decrease in testosterone would equate with a reduction in passion and arousal. But let's slow down a little bit. Testosterone levels do indeed decrease for many men as they get older, but they are also known to fluctuate throughout the day. Testosterone is also sensitive to environmental cues. Thus a new passionate relationship may increase testosterone levels, and a relationship that is past its passionate period may reduce those levels. It may be that the status of a relationship has more of an effect on our testosterone than the other way round.

I know plenty of men who began testosterone supplementation, and while there was a consensus that it increased energy, sex drive, and frequency and firmness of erections, few reported that this increased their sense of arousal for their partners. Only those men who began testosterone supplementation for the purpose of engaging in better sexual relations with their partners reported improved relationships. The majority of men, however, found themselves cruising for sex once again or spending hours each week looking at Internet porn. Testosterone supplementation did increase sexual arousal, but not necessarily for the men with whom they already shared their lives.

Physical Attractiveness

Another factor that is known to play a part in the reduction of desire is a decline in physical attractiveness. In the gay male community, with its focus on youth, fitness, and beauty, many consider the loss of physical beauty a tragedy. In a poll for his book *Chasing Adonis* (2007), Tim Bergling found that 68 percent of respondents thought the gay male community was "way too hung up" on the way men look. But as we will see, males, regardless of sexual orientation, rank physical attractiveness as extremely important if not the most important characteristic for sexual partners.

Physical attractiveness does indeed influence passion. There are many men with a spouse or partner who gained weight, underwent surgery, or experienced a traumatic accident resulting in a changed physical appearance who grapple with the effects of bodily changes on their relationship. Still, most couples find that passion begins to fade fairly rapidly even when the appearance of the beloved hasn't changed since they met. As a therapist who is male and gay, I cannot help but notice when a beautiful man enters my office. And more than likely, his paramour will be of equal attractiveness. Yet in spite of their combined beauty, these men still face the challenge of lost passion. It might be difficult to imagine that the guy you masturbate to in your head, the guy whose beauty makes him just about unapproachable, might have a long-term lover who no longer has any interest in sex with him. You would do anything just to touch his body, yet the man he lives with has minimal interest in it anymore. But that is often what happens.

Sexual Inadequacies

Sometimes passion dissipates because the sex wasn't so hot to begin with. In my practice I have found that many young men feel a great deal of pressure with regard to sexual performance. And "performance" is indeed the perfect description: men tend to judge themselves and feel judged by their demonstration of unerring sexual prowess. But how realistic is this expectation? There is pervasive pressure for men to always be ready for sex, to initiate sexual contact, and to gain erections infallibly. Men hold expectations of instinctive sexual expertise in spite of limited prior experience, particularly those men who are beginning their sexual experimentation during the delayed adolescence of their twenties and thirties. The art of lovemaking is seen as a birthright, not as an acquired skill.

Of course, if a man recognizes that he can be less than stellar in sex, he can become hyper-aware of his performance. So many men are busy monitoring themselves in their heads while engaged in sexual activity ("Am I going to come too fast?" "Am I losing my erection?") that they cannot let loose and actually enjoy themselves. Two of the classic sexual problems that inhibit sexual enjoyment are performance anxiety and spectatoring—watching oneself have sex instead of enjoying the act—and both without doubt can impede intimacy.

While all men have encountered expectations to be a perfect lover, the expectation is even more pronounced in the gay male community. We all know that gay men live in a highly sexualized environment, and this undoubtedly has an effect on our own sexual beliefs and assumptions. Many gay men have set standards so high for themselves in regards to sexual activity that it is no wonder that they and their partners are dissatisfied.

My personal favorite example of this occurred in the bathroom of a seedy bar—and believe me, I do mean seedy. My client followed a beckoning young adult into the stall and began to fondle his penis. The young man ejaculated within seconds, after which he apologized for his performance. "Usually I can last longer than that," he explained. Putting aside the fact that he wasn't being timed, what actually is the "appropriate" amount of time it should take for a male to ejaculate in an anonymous sexual encounter in a public bathroom with the risk of discovery quite high? Is there even a protocol or measurement to compare this to? Do we actually have to apologize for performance in even anonymous encounters? If this man had ejaculated onto my client's shoes or shirt, an apology is understandable. But not for timing. Other gay men with whom I shared this anecdote don't feel the same way. The typical response is to regale me with their own sexual adventures in which an anonymous contact was able to keep it "going for hours" or, like the young college man in the bathroom stall, came within seconds. The former group is spoken of with awe; the latter, derision. The fact that gay men feel compelled to show sexual expertise in even anonymous encounters is indicative of the pressures we put upon ourselves.

Such personal expectations of consistent sexual expertise can lead couples to find sex less than incredible and maybe even disappointing. If a couple, no matter how much they are in love, continue to have bad or unfulfilling sex, they have entered a negative trajectory. One or both of the men may disengage from the act altogether.

Underlying Assumptions about Sex

I often give couples a survey examining their beliefs, values, and assumptions about sex and sexuality, but ask the partners to complete the information separately. It is rare that at least one or two surprising differences don't arise. Couples tend to believe that they share the same sexual values, but such assumptions are problematic, particularly as passionate infatuation fades and each person reveals aspects of himself that he kept hidden during the early courtship stages. One would naturally think that in a relationship between two men, there would be values and attitudes mutually shared simply because of the similarity of the biological sex. I have been informed by many straight men of their belief that it must be easier for two men to live together than a man and a woman. But as we have seen, gay men enter relationships with shared gender expectations that are often destructive to compatibility—and, in addition, we cannot assume that any two males share the same underlying beliefs and assumptions.

Some of the sexual issues that male couples must explore and not simply take for granted include the acceptability of masturbation, anal sex, pornography, frequency of sex, and the decision as to who is the person to initiate sexual activity. Some males are proud of their sexual minority status and strike a defiant stance against heterosexual norms, while their partners may be much more closeted. Some men have been raised with a belief that sexual activity is "wrong" regardless of their orientation. For some of those men raised in particularly religious households, sex is solely designated for the purpose of procreation and is considered a duty rather than an opportunity for pleasure and intimacy. Other men may have a history of sexual abuse as children or have had repeated bad experiences with sex; both accumulate to form a belief that sexual passion leads inexorably to some type of physical and psychological pain.

Fortunately, the sexual arousal that comes with passion is often sufficient to hide the emotional baggage that each one of us carries into a new relationship. And even for the man who does take note of his concerns with a new partner, he will usually overlook them in the brain-induced delirious optimism that accompanies passion. "We'll get through this together" is the common refrain.

The Stressors of Daily Life

Stress and unresolved issues between two men in a relationship affect sex, and sexologists working with couples often use sexual activity as a barometer of relationship health. If a relationship is experiencing stress and conflict, one of the first signs is a loss of interest in sex with one's partner. Sometimes the refusal to have sex is strategically maneuvered by one partner in order to show his anger over this or that concern. Other times, smoldering resentment may make the thought of sex or even the simple touching of one's partner unbearable. But a loss of passion may stem from issues external to the relationship itself. The responsibilities of daily life that we were so willing to forgo while in passionate love may come crashing down around us. We may need to take care of children, an aging parent, or face a sudden upheaval in life such as an unexpected job loss. The daily strains of life may necessitate that we focus our attention elsewhere, or we may be too exhausted after a long day or week to even spark an interest in sex. Sexual passion wanes as other priorities in life make their presence felt.

Sexual Boredom and Companionate Love

At this point we have a catalogued a host of reasons why sizzling passion decreases, including changes in testosterone levels, changes in physical attractiveness, a deficit of lovemaking skills that leaves one or both partners unsatisfied, performance anxiety, spectatoring, fundamental differences in sexual expectations and assumptions between partners, unresolved issues from the past, relationship conflict and stress, and, finally, the daily stressors of life. And while each of these can indeed affect our sexual desire, in the early stages of a relationship, during that period when the conflux of hormones and neurochemicals forms a torrent, even these challenges can be conquered. Passion leads to an increase in testosterone. Excess energy helps us deal with stress. Sexual inadequacies and differences are overlooked. Yet there is still one more quite profound and yet all too common reason for the loss of sexual desire that occurs within a relationship: habituation and boredom.

In my very first class in human sexuality, the instructor was questioned by one of the students as to the most challenging sexual problem that she had to deal with in her clinical practice. Her response was a lack of sexual desire between individuals in a couple. How do you help a person become sexually aroused to something that once but no longer offers a source of sexual satisfaction? In her experience, one could treat many of the attending issues that surround a lack of sexual desire in a couple and hopefully find an intervention that had at least a minimal effect on either the quantity or quality of their sexual activity. However, boredom was more often than not something that could not be overcome. Sure, one could attend a weekend seminar on couples' sexual enrichment or rent an instructional video on co-creating a new sexual script, but in spite of the most elaborate of role-plays and expensive of props, boredom and the idea that "I've been here and done that" continues to haunt the fringes.

In *He's Just Not Up for It Anymore* (2008), Bob Berkowitz and Susan Yager-Berkowitz surveyed more than 4,000 men and women in relationships that had ceased to be sexual. And though the participants were heterosexual, the results replicate the same themes found in male relationships. Of the five top reasons men gave for ceasing sexual activity within a relationship, four centered on boredom.

Reason One: She isn't sexually adventurous enough for me.
Reason Two: She doesn't seem to enjoy sex.
Reason Three: I am interested in sex with others, but not with my wife.
Reason Four: I am angry at her.
Reason Five: I'm bored.

The authors noted that men tended to shift blame for their sexless relationships onto their partners. The Berkowitzes' response is, "It is difficult to believe that this lack of erotic excitement is completely one-sided, and that these men who identify their wives as unadventurous are themselves imaginatively passionate guys."

Drug makers, of course, are formulating new pharmaceutical interventions to fill this void. The most recognized, Viagra and related drugs, do not actually increase desire but rather make it more possible to be aroused. But companies are now experimenting with drugs that directly increase desire, or in other words, pharmaceutical aphrodisiacs. In females, testosterone supplementation has shown evidence of increasing sexual desire. Nevertheless, it is important to remember that an increase in desire does not necessarily mean an increase in desire for one's partner.

Sexual boredom is indeed a recognized effect in long-term relationships; we simply grow accustomed to a lover and his routine and even his body, no matter how perfect it may be. When looking at pornography on the Internet, I am always amused at the feedback other men offer in response to certain pictures: "I could suck this man's dick forever" or "I would never let him out of my bed." Really? I assure you that you would let him out of your bed at some point in the near future, no matter how wonderful and Adonis-like a physique he had. Sexual titillation dissipates, and we relentlessly and irrevocably tire of our sexual partners even when we love them dearly. The Berkowitzes' study on sexless marriages led them to conclude, "The constant, relentless, delicious sex of those first few months or years will probably never return. For the majority of people fortunate enough to be in loving long-term committed relationships, fantasies, vacations, and lacy underwear aren't going to reverse those brain chemicals back to the good old days."

Since passion and sexual desire are so much a function of the brain, a question at this point is whether there is an underlying physiological reason that leads to habituation. "The decline of romantic love is undoubtedly evolution's doing," Helen Fisher wrote in "Why We Love—the Nature and Chemistry of Romantic Love." "Intense romantic passion consumes enormous time and energy. And it would be decidedly disruptive to one's peace of mind and daily activities to spend years obsessively doting on a lover. Instead, the brain circuitry evolved primarily for one purpose: to drive our forebears to seek and find special mating partners, then copulate exclusively with 'him' or 'her' until conception was assured. At that point, ancestral couples needed to stop focusing on each other and start building a safe social world where they could rear their precious child together. Nature gave us passion. Then she gave us peace—until we fall in love again."

In her article on love in the February 2006 issue of *National Geographic*, Lauren Slater offers us a similar explanation: "Biologically speaking, the reasons romantic love fades may be found in the way our brains respond to the surge and pulse of dopamine that accompanies passion and makes us fly. Cocaine users describe the phenomenon of tolerance: The brain adapts to the excessive input of the drug . . .Maybe it's a good thing that romance fizzles. Would we build railroad, bridges, planes, faxes, vaccines, and television if we were always besotted? In place of the ever-evolving technology that has marked human culture from its earliest tool use, we would have instead only bonbons, bouquets, and birth control. More seriously, if the chemically altered state induced by romantic love is akin to mental illness or a drug-induced euphoria, exposing yourself for too long could result in psychological damage."

One couple succinctly told *The Advocate* of the changing role sex has played in their shared lives together: "Hot passion is great, but if it stayed that way for 20 years, we'd be exhausted! Sex now is different." A therapist interviewed for that same 1998 article recommended this solution: replacing the words "hot" and "sexy" with "comfortable" and "creative."

Many men do not accept habituation and a transition from "hot" and "sexy" to "comfortable" and "creative" without a fight. Some may brave the aisles searching for a self-help book on improving their sex lives or seek out the consultation of a sex therapist. In an ideal intervention, couples would examine the plethora of issues in their sexual relationship, and the result would likely be an improved sex life. But what would not occur is a return to the passionate heights of arousal experienced early in the relationship. A man may grow to love his partner even more and even enjoy sexual activity with him. But even the best intervention will not result in a greatly increased sex drive for his current partner.

If each couple is destined to lose and be unable to recapture the sexual heights, passion, and arousal that demarcate the early stages of a relationship, how should we envision a future for relationships? Research finds that many couples cross over into a new phase of intimacy called companionate love. In contrast to the idealization, lust, and preoccupation with one's lover in the passionate stage, companionate love is instead rooted in affection and commitment. Companionate lovers understand each other, trust each other, and are forgiving of each other's foibles. In short, companionate lovers are each other's best friends. Sexual passion and the relentless need to be with our partner each and every hour of the day is slowly overtaken by the warm fuzzy feelings that are far less disturbing to our day-to-day routines.

Many professionals believe that for a long-term relationship to survive, a couple must pass through the near-mystical experience of passion and become companionate lovers. Some lucky couples may maintain a sexual interest in each other for their entire lives, but for the majority, companionate love and the security it creates is a surefire step toward even more habituation and boredom. Companionate couples love each other and will sacrifice for each other, but they do not necessarily find each other sexually enticing. Viagra and related drugs may make it possible to continue to function sexually with a partner when one is not particularly interested, and drugs to induce desire may even stoke a temporary and muted flame of passion for one's lover again, but except for those rare couples, sexual passion is not likely to resurge.

It is at this point that I ask readers to purposefully question their own assumptions and expectations about relationships. If you are in a new relationship and are expecting it to maintain the sexual heights that you are feeling now, prepare for disappointment. However, as I believe that most readers of this text are not those passionately engrossed in a new love but rather those considering nonmonogamy to regain the sexual edge that has disappeared from a long-term relationship or those whose partner has engaged in nonmonogamy already, it is very important to question your expectations.

Let's present a hypothetical scenario. A drug company releases a new pharmaceutical that increases not only sexual arousal (the ability to maintain an erection) but also one that affects desire. This new drug is a modern equivalent to a love potion in that it increases sexual desire for the person you are already with. In short, you remain passionately in love, including sexual desire, for one's current partner and sexual boredom with this person is impossible. There would be no desire for any other male. Such a drug could cause our entire economy to crash as people fled their offices early or called in sick for days on end to stay in bed and have sex. But we'll assume that this drug makes it through clinical trials and receives FDA approval. Would you take it? Would you be willing to forgo a lifetime of sexual experiences with different people? Are you willing to give up sexual variety?

The men I have asked this question of have responded in the expected ways. A small minority says they would absolutely take this medication. The remainder was either steadfastly against such a medication or would have to seriously weigh the benefits against the drawbacks. In fact, the comment that I heard most often was that they would not take the drug but would be more than willing to give it to their current partners and spouses. For many men, the thought of losing a taste for sexual variety, of voluntarily giving up the ability to stroke another man's penis or even the daydreams and sexual fantasies of beautiful young men that accompany masturbation would be too much of a loss. The desire for sexual novelty and variety is just too primordial and profound an instinct for males for them to contemplate a life without it.

But there is no such drug, so the question is purely hypothetical. But the broader question remains: Are you willing to allow yourself to commit to a relationship that will lose sexual passion? Can you remain sexually monogamous when habituation and boredom set in? In short, are you willing to accept the inevitable transformation from passionate love to companionate love?

I find that a host of factors affect the answer to this second question. Personality factors such as risk-taking and a low tolerance for boredom, relationship factors such as the current sexual satisfaction level of the couple, length of time together as a couple, the dynamics of a relationship, and individual factors such as one's sexual beliefs, age, and past sexual experiences all influence the response. Still, the answers parallel those of the first question. Most men, regardless of how much they love and admire their partner, cannot foresee a future where they are willing to voluntarily abdicate sexual passion, even if this passion comes in small doses in the form of masturbation or, better yet, occasional dalliances with a third person.

The desire for sexual variety and novelty and the ability to quickly become bored with one's current sexual partner is built into the male brain. Whether this was stamped into our psyche through social conditioning or is an evolutionary artifact of an instinct that aided our species' survival (there is evidence for both), changes nothing: the desire exists in men and shapes male sexuality. What does that mean for gay male monogamy?

CHAPTER 5
Male Sexuality

THE GREATER OUR UNDERSTANDING of male sexuality, the greater our understanding of gay male sexuality—and that in turn will enable us to make informed decisions about monogamy and sexual non-exclusivity in our own lives.

Love and Monogamy as a Choice?

One of the best clinical tools I learned as a therapist was hypnosis, and a common example used in hypnosis training involves a post-hypnotic suggestion for an individual to open and close a window every time the hypnotist yawns. When the subject awakens from the trance, all he remembers is a comfortable sleep. Yet when the hypnotist yawns, the subject has an uncontrollable urge to go to the window and open it. If asked why he has just leapt from his chair to rush to the nearest window, he doesn't answer that the hypnotist told him to—indeed, he has no memory of the suggestion at all. Instead he will confabulate a reason for his action, most likely that "the room is too hot" or "I need some air."

As a therapist working from the school of thought that promotes the concept of free will, choice, and responsibility for decisions, I am nevertheless confronted by the reality that many of our decisions are not formulated consciously. Science presents us with more and more evidence that we are far less in control than we think we are. Sometimes, or maybe even most of the time, what we choose for our lives is based on unconscious processing, our decisions affected by profound and meaningful influences that remain below our conscious radar screens. We believe we know why we are performing this or that action, but our rationales are as fatuous as those given by the post-hypnotic subject as to why he is suddenly compelled to open a window.

We have a sexual repertoire that has evolved along with the human species. For example, most straight men rate younger women as more attractive than older women. Is this just a fluke of development, or did it ensure the ongoing survival of our species? A group of our early human ancestors may well have been attracted to gray-haired older women, but these women were also past their childbearing years. Thus this group would not have had much chance of successfully passing their genes on to the next generation. Putting aside the fact that we have yet to determine an evolutionary basis for homosexuality, we can safely assert that every male is the recipient of genes that both prime and activate his sexuality. These hardwired sexual traits play a major role in our sexual functioning, but in our assertions that we "know ourselves," and secure in our belief in our own self-awareness, we either underestimate their integral role in our sexual functioning or remain completely oblivious of their powerful influence. Like that hypnotized subject, we make excuses for what is otherwise inexplicable behavior that has been shaped over millions of years.

Lessons from *To Catch a Predator*

One of the most fascinating shows to appear on television over the past decade is *To Catch a Predator*. For those readers who haven't had the opportunity to watch this addictive series, it offers the chance to learn whether your coworker, friend, neighbor, priest or rabbi, son, or even husband is a child molester. A sting operation is set up in which an adult decoy acting as a pubescent male or female portrays himself as sexually available over the Internet. Within minutes, interested adults begin flooding the decoy with overtures. Some men remain strictly in the cyber-world, and their contact consists of messages ranging from vaguely sexual to graphically explicit, including nude photographs of themselves (with a particular tendency to send pictures of genitals). Many follow up by arranging to visit the home of the "teen," and this is where *To Catch a Predator* becomes mesmerizing. Men arrive at the homes of the ostensible teenager, often bringing alcohol, condoms, and pornography. Little do they know that they are on surveillance television the entire time. Once greeted at the door by an actor playing the role of the teenager who then quickly leaves the room with an excuse such as changing into swimwear, the adult male is unceremoniously greeted by the show's host in what becomes a very dark version of *Candid Camera*.

Viewers have seen males of all ages, from young adults to the elderly, from all socioeconomic classes, of all ethnicities, and even different sexual persuasions make excuses for their behavior, get a surprise tackling by hidden police officers, get handcuffed, and be removed to a mobile police headquarters for booking. Men even admit to having seen the series, yet still they come, searching for nubile flesh. These same men, upon recognizing that their lives are about to be destroyed on national television, refuse to leave the house; they know that once they exit a phalanx of burly officers will be waiting for them.

What readers haven't seen, however, are female offenders. Each episode presents us with male after male responding to the enticing possibility of sexual activity with a teenager, but a female never appears. In fact, the producers of the series offer a listing of every person caught in the operation on its Web site; not one female is on that list.

To Catch a Predator is a cultural artifact of the sexual differences between men and women. Over the past decade and a half a plethora of books, some of them best sellers, have tried to create typologies for male and female romantic and sexual behaviors and offer explanations based on genetic and evolutionary differences. This book is not particularly concerned with sexual and romantic differences between men and women, though we will avail ourselves of certain facts and inferences as they are relevant to our examination of monogamy.

However, the differences between gay men and straight men is most certainly relevant for our discussion, and what research, observation, and lived experience tells us is that there really isn't much difference between the two. In the last chapter we saw that all men, regardless of sexual orientation, could experience medical problems that affect sex, performance anxiety, spectatoring, and dissatisfaction in sex lives. Indeed, gay men and straight men are pretty much interchangeable with regard to sexual desire, arousal, and orgasm. The objects of desire may be different, but the underlying physiological and psychological processing that occurs is identical.

In an article on sexual activity in local, state, and federal park systems, I interviewed officials and rangers about their understanding of the issue. There tended to be an agreement that gay male cruising was more blatant and had a greater impact on park visitors in comparison to heterosexual sexual activity. However, one interviewee offered quite a profound appraisal. He believed that if straight men could avail themselves of settings such as parks where women too would engage in free and anonymous sexual activity, we would see a great many more heterosexual males cruising parks. If there were a park where women offered free oral sex, we could safely wager that the spot would become just as popular for straight men as Ridley Creek Park outside my hometown of Philadelphia is for gay men. (Incidentally, in 2006, Pennsylvania state representative Thomas Killion introduced legislation to call for stricter penalties for lewd behavior on public property after the highly publicized arrests of thirty-seven males soliciting sex from undercover rangers at the park.).

In truth, *To Catch a Predator* offers evidence that straight men will troll for sex in a similar fashion to gay men if given the opportunity; some drove hours and hundreds of miles for the chance. Research, too, finds similarities between gay and straight men and informs us that much of what we see in gay culture in connection with anonymous sexual activity with a variety of partners would be far more prevalent for straight men if only women would play along. Women act as restraints on straight male sexuality, and if they were to suddenly take a predilection to uncommitted and anonymous sexual activity, the ostensible differences between gay and straight men would be negligible.

Erotic Plasticity

Erotic plasticity is a relatively new concept in the field of sexology and is generally understood as the malleability of our sexuality to be influenced by environmental, social, and situational factors. Research finds that men exhibit far less erotic plasticity in comparison to females; female sexuality is greatly influenced by cultural and social factors, while male sexuality is generated more by hardwired factors such as genes and hormones

The evidence for hardwired male sexuality is intriguing, and again our basis of comparison is females. Lesbians are far more likely than gay men to have had past heterosexual sexual involvement, and are far more likely to become involved in this activity even after years of living an exclusively gay lifestyle. Yes, there are straight men that are gay for a day, and we have all heard that the difference between a gay men and a straight man is three strong drinks. But the evidence says otherwise; gay men do not report as much sexual activity with females and rarely voluntarily take on a straight lifestyle after living as a gay man. A male's sexual preference and sexual interests begin to emerge early in life, and once established, rarely fluctuate. Women demonstrate a far greater ability to modify sexual interests.

In addition, male sexual output tends to be more constant and less variable than it is in females. As an example, when a relationship ends for a woman, her sexual behaviors may shift suddenly from a satisfying and frequent sex life to one that evidences no sexual activity at all. This diminished output can last from months to years. Males, in contrast, tend to compensate for the loss of a relationship and the sexual activity that it entailed by increasing masturbation and engagement with casual sex partners.

Finally, education, religion, peers, and parents generally have more of an influence on a woman's sexual behavior than they do on that of men. And as we have already seen from laboratory research on arousal, male sexuality is hardwired and is not easily modified. The underlying aspects of male sexuality occur across cultures and remain resistant to even the most coercive efforts at change. It is these hardwired characteristics that shape the male perspective on and inclinations for nonmonogamy.

In comparison to females, males habituate (become bored) in sexual relationships quicker, are prone to seek out sexual novelty, desire a greater number of sexual partners, and are inclined to place much more value on youth and beauty. It should be obvious that such a discrepancy between the sexes offers many opportunities for conflict, but even in a same-sex relationship, problems are inevitable based on men's not particularly plastic sexual traits.

Youth and Beauty

What do straight men find most appealing and attractive in females? Research has found a number of characteristics, but all can be subsumed under the three categories of health, beauty, and youth. Based on our understanding that straight and gay men share the same hardwired sexual traits, it shouldn't come as a surprise that these same categories are identical for gay men. Readers who were sexually active during the height of the AIDS epidemic may recall agreeing to have some form of safe sexual involvement with a man we knew to be infected; it seemed worth it, as long as he was attractive, or better yet, hot.

But once the ravages of the disease became evident, particularly the presence of lesions and weight loss, our sexual desire for that person disappeared. Men are not necessarily turned off by ill health; only by overt indications of it. It is a sexual rarity for men to find indications of poor health a signal for desire.

As for age and beauty, it is impossible to deny that culture has some effect on prevailing standards of beauty, for example, changing fads for thin versus voluptuous women. However, every culture worldwide finds youth and beauty the most salient traits for sexual partners. When asked to rank photographs of men and women differing in age in order of physical attractiveness, both gay and straight males consistently rank the youngest as the most attractive. Similarly, a study of personal ads found that both groups of men place a high premium on physical attractiveness and even on very particular physical attributes (e.g., breast size and penis size); this is in contrast to those ads placed by heterosexual females and lesbians. Women tend to seek men who are already successful or who have the potential for success, are physically attractive, offer evidence of a firm commitment, and are kind and intelligent. Of these four characteristics, women are most willing to allow physical attractiveness to be a luxury rather than a necessity. Men, on the other hand, seek the same combination of traits as women but rank their importance differently. Physical attractiveness is not a luxury but an essential for males. Indeed, men are willing to accept a woman with a less than pleasing personality and little potential for success as long as she is attractive and offers evidence of commitment.

The use of physical attractiveness as "bait" occurs in our own gay world version of *To Catch a Predator*. However, instead of a decoy posing as a young underage male, we have gay men posting pictures of themselves either taken twenty years ago or, better yet, of a completely different person that most would classify as a stud. My friend Ronald began an online dialogue with a gentleman that led to an exchange of pictures. Now Ronald admitted to sending a photograph of himself taken six years earlier and in the most flattering of light. But at least it was him and fairly recent. His online paramour reciprocated with a picture of an imposing and jaw dropping oh-so-hot twenty-something. Ronald couldn't believe his luck and couldn't wait to both meet and be fucked by this person. As he proudly taunted his friends with this picture, one pointed out that it bore a resemblance to an actor in male pornography. Ronald of course denied this as he already knew that his new Internet friend was a high-school teacher. His friends recognized the futility of attempting to dissuade him of his belief and sat back and waited for the inevitable. Some really did hope that the man in the picture was the same person in real life; they wanted to be next in line in case he and Ronald didn't hit it off.

On the night of the arranged meeting, Ronald responded to the ringing of the doorbell at his apartment with a guise of calmness that barely hid his breathless anticipation. But when he opened the door, Ronald didn't recognize the person standing there; instead of a twenty-year-old with pecs that elicited involuntary salivation, there stood a middle-aged balding man with a noticeable paunch. The schoolteacher had used a picture of a porn actor; he explained that this was the only way he found that he could attract other males. In the case of Ronald, a picture of a hot male he believed to be available so intoxicated him that he simply threw his common sense out the window. In the case of the imposter, youth and beauty were the only characteristics that he found infallible for meeting other gay men.

By the way, how do you think Ronald responded to the stranger at his door? Many men would have slammed the door in his face. Others, though, say to themselves, "What the hell. You're already here." Ronald is in this latter category, and he invited his Internet pen pal in for sex. This willingness to engage in casual sexual activity even when not necessarily attracted to the other person is yet another behavior with deep hardwired roots.

Casual Sex

> The picture is not a very pretty one, but humans were not designed by natural selection to coexist in matrimonial bliss. They were designed for individual survival and genetic reproduction. The psychological mechanisms fashioned by these ruthless criteria are often selfish ones. (Buss, 2003, p. 152)

> Unless we're going to argue that we were dumped here by space aliens and operate totally differently from every other species on earth, we have to accept that, as with every other species, biology plays a role in our behavior. It's not an "if," but a "how," and "how much." (Blum, 1997, p. 267)

A 1994 study asked male and female participants what amount of time they would have to know someone before engaging in sex with him or her. Five years? Two years? A month? A week? Most women would not even consider having sex with another person unless they had known each other for at least several months. In contrast, males would have sexual contact based on a week's acquaintance. Some would even engage in sexual contact based on an hour of time together. In another study, researchers played audiotapes of conversations for both male and female college students. Some of these conversations were explicitly sexual, while others dealt with mundane topics such as the advantages and disadvantages of choosing one major over another. Most of the research participants found the erotic dialogues sexually stimulating. However, only the men found the mundane topics sexually stimulating. Indeed, many of the men exhibited more physiological arousal to these latter conversations than females did to the erotic dialogues.

In one of my personal favorite studies, attractive males and females were hired to approach strangers on a busy college campus. Upon approaching a stranger, these confederates were trained to say, "I have been noticing you around campus. I find you very attractive," and then ask one of three questions: (1) Would you go out with me tonight? (2) Would you come over to my apartment tonight? and (3) Would you go to bed with me tonight? What do you think the results were for males? Sixty-nine percent of males consented to visit the person's apartment, while, in contrast, only six percent of females were so obliging. None of the women consented to have sex, but seventy-five percent of the males did. "In humans, the male system seems so jittery with sexual readiness that just about anything—high-heeled shoes, a smile, a friendly conversation—will produce a sexual response" (Blum, 1997, p. 228).

Research, polls, surveys, and even laboratory studies all reveal similar information about male sexuality. Men are more easily sexually aroused than women, are sexually aroused to a wider variety of objects and circumstances, desire a greater number of sexual partners, and are far more willing to engage in casual sex. Additionally, in quantity, males have more sexual fantasies, daydreams, and even nocturnal sexual dreams than females. Not surprisingly, the majority of pornography and prostitution services cater to males. Male sexuality is indeed different from female sexuality, and all of these same character-istics are applicable to gay men.

In sum, the ongoing continuity of a species entails not only survival against the daily travails and threats to existence but also the creation of new generations. Thus we have been shaped by nature to be extremely sexual beings; males in par-ticular are wired to frequently seek out opportunities to dis-seminate their seed. Recall the example of hypnosis offered ear-lier. Even though men have been shaped by evolution to seek out frequent and varied sexual partners, this does not imply conscious awareness of the process. Alexander does not go out to the bar on a Saturday saying to himself that his genes are in-fluencing his decision to seek out a good-looking male for an evening's activity. He goes about his business oblivious to the fact that his sexual longings are the outcome of millions of years of evolution. Nor does hardwired sexuality imply that we have no control over our behaviors. To cheat on one's partner and blame it on one's genes is patently ridiculous. We do have control over our sexual responses, but nature has created this to be an often-titanic struggle, and just as often we don't want to exert the effort and would rather partake of the brief sexual pleasure that comes with a temporary liaison.

Learning to Be Masculine

In his fascinating cultural history of the penis, *A Mind of Its Own* (2001), David Friedman writes that our previous understanding of male sexuality and masculinity is now archaic. "A man is no longer measured by his physical strength—his ability to build shelter for his family, fight in hand-to-hand combat, or draw water from a well. Machines do that for him. Muscles are more symbolic than useful. So the erect penis has become the more powerfully symbolic 'muscle' of them all" (pp. 304–305).

Males are inculcated with a specific image of masculinity in our culture, and those who step outside of these restrictive parameters are the recipients of disapproval from families, peers, and, in most cases, the world at large. Several of the characteristics of this narrow male gender role include the need to avoid displays of femininity or feminine interests, to exhibit self-reliance and aggression in meeting one's own needs, to focus on the importance of achievement and status over that of affiliation with others, to restrict emotionality, and to maintain an orientation toward sex that minimizes its relational aspect with partners.

Male socialization creates men who are uncomfortable with intimacy, coupled with a directive to be as sexually active as possible. Males are taught from an early age that "scoring" with a number of partners is the one true indication of masculinity, and this belief then remains prevalent throughout a lifetime. In addition, males may not learn how to connect to other people intimately and can even be shunned for such displays; empathy and perspective-taking skills are generally not taught and seen as unimportant for young boys.

When a male reaches the age of puberty and is plunged into a morass of sexual interests and sensations, the desire for sexual contact with another person stands in stark contrast with his learned need to be self-reliant and to refrain from signs of tenderness and emotionality. Young men often approach sex as they have been taught to approach most domains in their lives, with aggression and instrumentality. Get the job done and don't value the feelings of a partner; what matters is sexual performance. It is only through non-connected sexual adventures that males can turn into men.

It is an uncontested fact that we need intimate relationships—those in which we trust another person enough to make ourselves vulnerable—for optimal physical and psychological health. Since males are often taught that vulnerability is a weakness, sometimes the only intimacy that occurs in a man's life is through sexual contact with another person. But even then, males do not open themselves up to partners and they maintain an emotional distance, thus never allowing themselves to really get to know another person. They instead worry about sexual performance. One result of this can be that when men do begin to experience intimacy with another person, the overwhelming trepidation that accompanies this sensation results in the need to distance themselves.

We cannot take it for granted that young men, whatever their sexual orientation, will grow into adults capable of intimacy, defined here not just as sexual intimacy but also the ability to be emotionally secure with another person. For males who fail to learn intimacy, a series of repercussions will follow, including superficial relationships, an increased likelihood of engaging in affairs and anonymous sexual activity, and a probability that committed relationships will be of brief duration. Sadly, when biological sexual urges are imprinted with societal expectations concerning acceptable codes of masculinity, we find relationships with little intimacy enjoined with a need for physical gratification often met with pornography, masturbation, and sexual affairs.

CHAPTER 6

The Process of Infidelity

IN PREPARING THIS CHAPTER, I received a fair bit of criticism for the use of such words as "infidelity," "unfaithful," and "cheating," and it was suggested that I instead use the less loaded but more unwieldy phrase "violation of a sexual agreement." Writer and therapist Michael Bettinger makes a salient point that the former words imply a victimizer and a victim, and in real life such clear differentiations are rare. In her book *Lust in Translation* (2007), a study of infidelity from a cross-cultural perspective, Pamela Druckerman makes a similar point to Bettinger: "There's no empirical evidence that people who are sexually faithful make better doctors, business partners, citizens, or presidents. Likewise, there's no proof that people who have extramarital sex embezzle money more often, commit more murders, tell more lies, or are generally more corrupt than those who are faithful. . . . The belief that cheating on your spouse is part of a constellation of character flaws and misbehaviors may be true, but it hasn't been tested." It is understandably tempting to rely on unrealistic images of the innocent betrayed victim and the guilty nefarious cheating spouse, but most incidents of infidelity are far more complicated than this simplistic dichotomy.

I sent out e-mail queries to some notable figures in the

study of infidelity with specific questions for this chapter. My first question was, "In your practice, what is the most common type of 'affair' you encounter with coupled gay men? One-night stands? Long-term affairs? Compulsive sexual activity with different partners?" It didn't take long before I realized that my question was too open to interpretation.

The very first response was from a well-known psychologist who has both worked extensively with and written about gay male relationships: "You use the term 'affairs.' Do you realize this is a value-laden word with an almost exclusively negative connotation used by heterosexuals to describe their nonmarital liaisons? This is a totally inappropriate word to use when describing what you are seeking to describe. The entire question reeks of lack of understanding of human sexuality and gay sexuality." Whoa, I thought to myself upon reading this, maybe I am totally confused about nonmonogamy and gay men.

After consideration of the first e-mail response and the input of other professionals who offered their assistance, I realized that even though my question was badly worded, the underlying sentiment was still valid: Gay men do "cheat" on their partners if they lead these partners to believe that they are monogamous when they really are not. Even more, if a man develops a sexual relationship with another person that is purposefully kept hidden from the primary partner, it's an affair, whether it's a fuck buddy or a long-term second lover. If both partners have agreed to an open relationship condoning additional sex partners and lovers, the use of the words "cheating" and "affair" are inappropriate—but they are entirely appropriate if one man is having sexual relations with another that is obfuscated through lies.

Don-David Lusterman, an expert on infidelity, wrote to me that in his experience, one-night stands were most common with male couples, while long-term affairs were the least prevalent. He also begins to look for issues of sexual compulsivity when he encounters a man who engages in repeated episodes of this particular type of activity. Dennis Debiak, professor of clinical psychology at Widener University, stated that in his clinical experience, gay men are increasingly engaged in cyber-affairs with other men online, but with no actual physical contact taking place. Debiak told me that some already-partnered men create profiles on dating and hook-up sites in which they list themselves as "single" or "available," even though they deny actually meeting anybody for sex or even a date. Is this cheating? Is it a violation of a sexual agreement?

Dr. Frank Pittman, one of the most outspoken practitioners in the realm of infidelity studies, says, "The hallmark of infidelity is not necessarily sex, but secrecy . . .[and is] best defined as a betrayal of the couple's agreement about sexual and romantic entanglements" (2005, p. 136). He slyly suggests that those who may be confused as to whether their outside involvements constitute infidelity should ask their current spouse or partner for clarification. And in an overview of the research on infidelity, Hertlein, Wetchler, and Piercy (2005) postulate that "emotional intimacy with another person to the detriment of the primary relationship" can be considered infidelity (p. 6). Others in the field remind us that the word "infidelity" is no longer applied only to married couples, and gay men in relationships can indeed experience infidelity.

Why Do Gay Men Cheat?

We have already fundamentally answered the question "why men cheat." Here, though, I would like to delineate a more fine-tuned understanding of why this or that man cheats. All men have the capacity to be sexually unfaithful while in a committed relationship, and many gay men live in environments that offer an all-you-can-eat sexual buffet. Why is it then that some males can remain sexually faithful in a relationship for years, while others find such a promise arduous after only several months? Why does this man have copious sexual liaisons on a weekly basis while the other only engages in the activity once every several years? Of course, environment plays no small part. Those living in the gay ghetto have more opportunity for cruising and meeting other interested gay men than those presumably living in rural states where cows outnumber people. Still, I can introduce you to men who live in the gay ghetto and yet decline anonymous sexual activity, and I can introduce you to men who live in wooded cabins that haunt the highway rest stops at dawn or drive hundreds of miles for a sexual adventure that lasts less than an hour. There are indeed other factors at play, and this section sets out to explore them.

Personality

The likely best predictor for infidelity is if our partner has engaged in the activity in the past. Peter, for example, was shocked to discover that his partner, Lorne, had had sex with another person while on a business trip. Peter must have a short memory. If he stopped to contemplate the past for just several seconds, he might recall that he and Lorne had become a couple while Lorne had been involved in a three-year-long relationship with another man. Michael LaSala, the author of several well-considered articles on gay male monogamy, reminded me that each person's sexual history is indicative of satisfaction with monogamy. "In my experience," he said, "men who have had a lot of casual sex when they are single and are having trouble maintaining a monogamous relationship are simply not meant to be monogamous—and that's ok. But they have to face it."

Personality, too, affects sexual behavior. Gay men who are easily bored and/or risk takers and who require adventure for satisfaction are often prone to seek sexual escapades outside of a partnership. All of us will eventually become bored sexually with our partners, but for those with a low tolerance for boredom, this could occur after only months in a relationship.

In addition to risk-taking and low tolerance for boredom, three other personality traits indicate a predisposition to sexual infidelity. First, a lack of empathy and indifference to the feelings of others. Second, a sense of entitlement. Third, acting on impulse. Of course, simply being a man is indicative of sexual infidelity, but those men who possess some combination of lack of empathy, entitlement, and impulsiveness are more likely to engage in more numerous affairs and earlier in a relationship. The more of these traits that a man possesses, the more he is likely to act quickly and without much consideration of consequences, disregard accepted rules for behavior, and feel entitled to have sex with whom he damn well pleases.

In studies, men who exhibit these characteristics admit that they are more likely to flirt, have one-night stands, and even simultaneous romantic relationships. Kareem, for example, had long become accustomed to Leroy's disregard of his feelings. Leroy constantly reneged on promises, allowed Kareem to shoulder almost all of the responsibility for their shared household, including cleaning and paying bills, and demonstrated apathy to any topic that didn't personally interest him. But when his mother became deathly ill, Kareem was devastated to learn that instead of offering expected solace, Leroy had invited a young male back to their household for sex while Kareem spent the night at his mother's bedside. Of course a relevant question is why the hell Kareem remained by such an asshole as Leroy, and thus Kareem has much to answer for. Regardless, Leroy exhibits indifference and entitlement, as is made plain by his sexual escapades.

Another characteristic is sexual compulsivity. Since the release of Patrick Carnes's work on sexual addictions in the early 1980s and the expanding availability of resources for this "condition" (*Cruise Control* by Robert Weiss was released in 2005 as a self-help book for gay men experiencing sexual compulsivity), we have seen an increasing recognition that a person can literally sexually lose control of himself. Carnes believes that sexual behavior becomes problematic when a male can no longer control it, continues in spite of adverse consequences, and spends an inordinate amount of time in trying to engage in the activity. So for example, if a male in a relationship finds that he cannot stop engaging in anonymous sex or is spending hours each day cruising in spite of legal and relationship repercussions, he might be experiencing a sexual addiction. Other researchers hesitate to call sexual compulsivity an addiction until we have a better understanding of the effects of sex on the brain, but they still acknowledge that for many individuals, certain sexual outlets can become recurrent, extreme, distressing, and interfere with daily functioning.

Still another personal characteristic that can seriously interfere with monogamy is substance use. Trying to remain monogamous while one or both partners is out partying and using crystal meth does not predict a stable relationship. Many drugs have an impact on sexual behaviors, and drug use before or during sex is associated with decreased inhibition and multiple sex partners. How does one commit to monogamy while concurrently using substances that compel a need for sexual activity with other and often numerous men?

Finally, and the weakest of predictors, the opinions that men hold about monogamy may indicate a propensity for infidelity. However, words often do not match actions, and there are men who hold a liberal view accepting of sexual infidelity yet do their best to refrain from it. In contrast, there are men who condemn sexual infidelity but still engage in affairs.

We see that there are a number of personality characteristics and traits predictive of nonmonogamy. The more of them a man displays, the more likely he is to be challenged by monogamy.

Relationship Quality

An accepted matrix for couples consists of four types. As you read their descriptions, guess which types would be most prone to sexual infidelity.

1. *Mutually Committed Relationships: A relationship in which both partners are committed to each other and have shared investments in the relationship that act as barriers to separation (e.g., a house, children, etc.).*
2. *Uncommitted Lovers: A relationship in which the two individuals love and are committed to each other but have no shared investments.*

3. *Loveless but Invested; The love two individuals had for each other has now dissipated but there are still shared investments that bar separation. Such a couple remains together for convenience or simply out of apathy.*

4. *The Stranger Relationship: There is no love and no shared investments. This is the couple most likely to separate.*

Readers may be forgiven for mistakenly thinking that the last two—loveless but invested and the stranger types—are the relationship types most likely to lead to infidelity. Surprisingly, the reality is that for men, all of the above can be riddled with infidelity. There is a clear division between males and females in regard to motivating factors for cheating. For women, the quality of the relationship is the most salient aspect, and when asked to list factors that might tempt them into an affair, women offer reasons centering on emotional factors such as love, intimacy, and companionship. For men though, the quality of the relationship has less bearing on extra-relational sex. One study looked for a link between marital dissatisfaction and sex occurring outside of the relationship. More than half of men ranked their current relationship as "very happy." When asked to list factors for infidelity on their part, men rarely mention emotional concerns similar to females but instead focus on the need for sexual novelty, variation, and an emotional "thrill." Males report feeling a strong commitment to their partners even while engaged in covert sexual activity.

There are relationship qualities that influence decisions of infidelity, but in general, they are not as much of a factor for men as sexual boredom. Both emotional instability and quarrelsomeness have been found to lead a partner to consider outside sexual liaisons. Feeling unloved, undervalued, neglected, or outright ignored are also relationship qualities that lead to affairs, as are extended periods of separation.

Quality of the Sexual Relationship

Sexual pleasure was not recognized as an important aspect of relationship quality prior to the Sexual Revolution of the 1960s and 1970s. Though marriages and long-term romantic relationships are rarely havens of bliss that are sometimes simply easier and healthier to end, such a sentiment rarely occurred to earlier generations. Even if it did, pressure from family, church, and society at large made such a decision feel shameful. Most couples just stuck it out until death with little expectation of enduring sexual satisfaction.

Today, though, largely due to the Sexual Revolution, we expect romance, passion, and spectacular sexual relationships, and the absence of any of those is a reason for terminating that relationship. We believe we shouldn't have to tolerate bad or even monotonous sex. Still, when we acknowledge that men quickly become bored with a sex partner, that one person cannot sexually satisfy us perpetually, and that we thrive on sexual novelty, we must accept that long-term sexual satisfaction remains a conundrum.

Types of Infidelity

There are several competing classification systems for infidelity, but the simplest and generally most well-accepted one contains only three categories. In this system, infidelity is motivated by one of the following:

1. *Sexual gratification*
2. *Emotional gratification*
3. *Both sexual and emotional gratification*

It will come as no surprise to most gay men that our infidelity is often based on sexual gratification and with little interest in emotional complications. We want exciting, satisfying, and recreational sex. Straight men too can appreciate this, but they soon learn that there is an exceedingly limited number of females willing to engage in recreational sex or without some type of emotional involvement. Gay men in contrast find that there is a surfeit of other gay males who not only want recreational sex and who have no desire for emotional entanglements. We get to have our cake and eat it too.

Consider the following examples:

- *Weslen and Donald have been a couple for seven years. Weslen's job requires much travel for days at a time. One evening he pulls over at a highway rest stop for a break and he notices a very attractive man standing outside the public bathroom. The young guy is really Weslen's physical type. After several minutes of evasive eye contact, Weslen follows him into the bathroom, enters a stall, gives him oral sex, and, finally, masturbates him to ejaculation. Both leave likely to never see each other again. In his seven years together with his partner Donald, this is the second time that Wes has engaged in sexual activity outside their relationship. He will not tell Donald, as his partner believes that they are a strictly monogamous couple.*
- *Ed and David have been a couple for seven years. For the past year, Ed has left work early two to three times per week*

to stop at a local state park that he passes on his commute home. The public bathroom is the focal point of much male-on-male sexual activity. Ed nods his acknowledgement to some of the other "regulars" in the parking lot, and he sits in his vehicle waiting for someone to make the first move to the bathroom. Often, nothing sexual happens, but Ed has still managed to receive oral sex and masturbate other men on five occasions in the past six months. He does not tell David, as his partner believes that they are a strictly monogamous couple.

- *Calvin and Josh have been a couple for seven years. Calvin freely admits that he knows very little about modern technology (he refuses to even carry a cell phone), but his friend tempts him with his description of a "steamy" all-male chat room. Calvin decides to pay a cyber visit one afternoon from his home office and becomes entranced with the site. It doesn't take long before he meets "Randy" and they begin an online friendship. He and Randy hit it off so well from the very beginning that Calvin begins to vouchsafe details from his personal life with Josh, including sexual aspects. Their messages become increasing sexualized, and Calvin begins to fantasize and even masturbate to images of Randy though they have never met in person, spoken by phone, or even exchanged pictures. Calvin does not tell Josh about his new "friendship" and certainly does not consider this cheating; he and Josh are monogamous.*
- *Alex has become sexually and emotionally involved with Angel though he already shares a life of seven years (including a house and mutual bank accounts) with Ronald. Though they have only known each other for eight months, Alex recognizes that he is widely infatuated with Angel and*

that this could have repercussions for his entire life. He has been untruthful with Ronald, making excuses for lateness and absences, his lack of desire for sex, and distractibility. Alex has increasing fantasies of leaving Ronald but is then swept with guilt. He is without doubt "torn between two lovers."

Based on the descriptive system presented thus far, we can label the first two scenarios as offering sexual gratification; the protagonists don't even find out the identities of their sexual partners. The third scenario, the triangle of Calvin, Josh, and Randy, is primarily one of emotional gratification in that Calvin feels he can share anything with Randy and he does do just that. There are indeed sexual aspects to their relationship, but since Calvin and Josh have not even learned what the other one looks like, let alone made physical contact, there will be many opinions as to whether that constitutes infidelity. Partners in a cyber-affair, their off-line partners, and professionals who work with gay men may all have different opinions. The impact of cyber-affairs is now a serious area of investigation, and we will have a better understanding of its complexity in the coming years. Commonly, the involved partner will deny infidelity since no physical contact is ever made. Their partners and many professionals counter this with their claim that any type of secret relationship that has an effect on the primary relationship is infidelity. Finally, the last scenario of Alex, Angel, and Ronald is a quintessential example of a combined emotional/gratification. This type of involvement is what most people label an "affair." And research tell us that the combined type poses the most threat to an established relationship and is the most difficult for the betraying partner to voluntarily end.

Other researchers have come up with more elaborate systems of categorizing infidelity; though we do not need to go in depth for these additional classification systems, they still offer some pertinent information. One of the classification systems created by psychologist Don-David Lusterman in his book *Infidelity: A Survival Guide* (1998) is appealingly simple and complements the sexual/emotional/combined type presented earlier. He too lists three separate categories. First, *one-night stands.* The sexual incident between Wes and the stranger at the highway rest stop is one such example. A one-night stand can occur unplanned, or it can be planned in advance, as with a man who goes off to the male cinema for some action. The next type Lusterman calls *philandering,* which he describes as a pattern of one-night stands and/or brief sexual flings with no emotional attachment. The second scenario, with Ed and David, is an illustration of philandering. Ed seeks sexual activity outside his relationship on a fairly consistent basis, an activity that has become part of his day-to-day life. The third type of infidelity is called an actual *affair,* in which one partner becomes emotionally and often sexually involved with a third person. This new relationship takes on increasing importance to the detriment to the original relationship. It is also kept hidden, and lies and secrets are used to maintain its invisibility from the betrayed partner.

The Internet relationship between Calvin and Randy would be classified as an affair by many, particularly if it is purposefully kept hidden and detracts from and/or damages the established relationship. The final scenario—the triad of Alex, Angel, and Ronald—is without doubt what the vast majority would call an affair.

We now have two classification systems that describe infidelity. Still, some professionals, including myself, are not satisfied with these two systems and call for a more finely delineated system, one that goes beyond the general label of motivation by emotional or sexual gratification.

So let's take all of this information and create an easily comprehendible typology for gay male couples and infidelity. These three categories clarify the underlying motivating factors for gay men and infidelity. Whether you are the man actually involved in extra-relational activity or you are the hurt partner waiting on the side, see which of these categories best describes your predicament.

I. Relationship Issues That Lead to Infidelity and Affairs

Blow (2005) mentions that he has never worked with a couple coping with infidelity who did not exhibit destructive levels of criticism, contempt, and defensiveness even before the infidelity began. Sometimes these problems may result in tirades, screaming matches, and, yes, broken dishes. Other times the couple tries to conceal the unhappiness or rage that lurks just beneath the surface, most often by avoiding or minimizing contact with each other. The problems could arise from the special set of issues so many gay men bring to a committed relationship while in the throes of passion. They wake from several months of sustained euphoria to realize that they don't even know the person they are now living with. This is the point when pitched relationship battles and dysphoria begin.

For the purposes of our classification, the first motivating factor for infidelity and affairs is a relationship that is not working. Infidelity is a symptom of deeper relationship issues.

II. Personal Issues That Lead to Infidelity and Affairs

This second category stems from the unresolved personal issues that cause one partner to seek out other men. If one partner has a serious problem—addiction, internalized homophobia, or a life crisis—both partners are ultimately affected. In this second category of motivations for gay men and infidelity, the primary cause rests with one of the men in the couple, though his partner is unavoidably affected. Some of the underlying issues in this second category include sexual compulsivity, substance use and abuse, internalized homophobia, a lack of empathy and indifference to the feelings of others, impulsivity, a sense of entitlement, and those who have been strongly inculcated with the prototypical masculine ideal of sexual conquest as a signifier of value and worth. Again, the motivational goal here is not to hurt one's partner, and it is not the relationship that is the core problem. It is the one partner, his issues, and their effect on the relationship that is the cause.

III. Male Desire for Sexual Novelty and Excitement

This last category for infidelity covers a partnership that is doing well, with both partners satisfied with the relationship, and no desire in either man for separation. Each man might have some complaints about the other—not unusual in a relationship that has passed its passionate stage—but they have learned how to work together and achieve a relationship that is a source of contentment and pleasure.

The motivating factor for infidelity here is sexual novelty. "I love my partner, but I'm SO bored sexually" is a common refrain from men who engage in infidelity in this last category. Passion has turned to companionate love, lust has disappeared, and sex, though possibly still pleasurable and satisfying, is missing that incendiary spark that evokes the spontaneous tremulous involvement of our brain, hormones, and penis. Men in this category who engage in infidelity are driven by the underlying genetic factors that program all of us to desire extra sexual activity. Harming a spouse is not a goal. These men may avail themselves of a sexual opportunity that wonderfully and unexpectedly arises (a 2004 study by Michael LaSala found that gay man engaged in infidelity simply because the opportunity presented itself). Others may plan on a visit to the steam room, male adult movie theater, or local park for some quick anonymous activity. Some men may have one and only one "one-night stand" throughout an entire relationship, others may have several, and still others may try to capture some sexual activity on the side whenever they can.

In reviewing the results of his poll of almost 1,000 gay men, Tim Belgling offers the following appraisal: "I'm not saying monogamy is impossible; I've seen it, it can work. I'm just saying it's pretty hard, so to speak, to stay 100 percent faithful to the same partner 100 percent of the time. And a lot of gay men I talked with question whether it's even desirable. They spoke of 'variety,' and 'spicing it up,' and told me how their sexual tastes have changed over time, so that while emotional monogamy might be something they seek, they don't pretend that they can be physically satisfied by sleeping with the same guy, night after night, year after year."

Let's summarize. Gay men will be become engaged in affairs and infidelity for three primary reasons: first, because they are unhappy in their relationships; second, because of unaddressed personal issues in one of the partners; third, sexual boredom and the quest for something new and exciting. There is no strict delineation between the categories—a couple can be confronted with all three.

Toby and Daniel, for example, find sexual activity less than stellar after ten years, and they have little dialogue between them. They are polite and kind to each other but have found themselves quite distant from each other over the past several years. Both men tend to refrain from discussing their feelings (after all, they were socialized all through their childhoods that real men don't show emotions or talk about them) until a serious argument occurs. At that point, the typical emotion expressed is anger. Even make-up sex isn't so hot anymore. Daniel makes a habit of going out on Saturday nights with *his* friends, often to a bar with male strippers. With the cajoling and support of his friends and after imbibing a number of mixed drinks, Daniel pays money so that he can give a dancer oral sex. This has happened twice in the past six months.

Affairs

Several questions come to mind when discussing affairs. Are all affairs motivated by relationship discontentment? Do I have to be unhappy with my first partner before I seek out an affair? Is it possible to love more than one person? A man may find himself in the enviable position of having two lovers to which he is both emotionally and sexually attached. (The other involved men may not be quite so pleased, though.) In most cases, the second relationship develops either from what was supposed to be an anonymous sexual encounter or out of a friendship in which sexual feelings develop.

Leo, for example, has been happily involved with Paul for five years though he occasionally partakes of a quick blowjob in the steam room at the predominantly gay gym near his workplace. One afternoon he slips out of the workplace to see a recently opened film. Once seated, he recognizes one of his more recent sexual involvements entering the theater, and they nod an acknowledgment to each other as he passes down the aisle. After the film, the other gentleman approaches him to ask how he liked the film. This is followed by an invitation to have coffee at Starbucks across the street. Numbers are exchanged, and before two months have gone by, Leo is feeling a passion for another man, a passion he hasn't felt in more than two years. While intoxicated with passion, Leo is still aware that his affair would be quite damaging to his relationship with Paul. He has no interest in hurting him but is now precariously balanced between two men. In Leo's case, as is typical with males, emotional attachment and the gratification that grows from it started out with sex. Occasional sexual contact can lead to entwined emotional involvement.

In another scenario, Aaron and Demetrius met at the gym and became spotting partners for each other. Both are happily involved with other men. Still, they are undeniably attracted to each other; in between sets they talk about their jobs, movies they have recently seen, their jobs, and even their relationships. Unbeknownst to each other, they have even masturbated to thoughts of each other. During one Friday morning workout, Aaron excitedly tells Demetrius that a small theater in the suburbs is showing an audience participation version of "Mommy

Dearest," a film dear to both men but whose camp appeal is lost on their partners. They decide to meet up for dinner and the show.

In this example, the sexual tension is apparent in the relationship. The men haven't engaged in any form of sexual activity with each other, but it might very well be heading that way. This is an example of a sexual relationship developing from a relationship that is purely platonic—at least at first.

Helen Fisher's research on the human brain found that we can indeed have great sexual attraction for a second person even while we are adamantly in love with another. We already know this from our daily experience, but Dr. Fisher goes on to explain that humans are capable of three types of love simultaneously: "It seems to be the destiny of humankind that we are neurobiologically able to love more than one person at a time. You can feel profound attachment for a long-term spouse, *while* you feel romantic passion for someone in the office or your social circle, *while* you feel the sex drive as you read a book, watch a movie, or do something else unrelated to either partner." In other words, we can have companionate love for our long-term partner, be infatuated with another man, and still masturbate to images of unapproachable males on a recently rented video, all at the same time.

There is no evidence that we are hardwired to only love one person at a time, and we could thus have two (or more) loving relationships. But there are several complications. Recall that our brain chemistry goes haywire while in the throes of infatuation. Men in affairs all too often think that they can somehow make the situation work out for all involved parties. "This can work, and I can keep everybody happy." Landers and Mainzer

(2005) state that just about everybody else can see that this gentleman is delusional, but in his own head he believes that a happy resolution is possible. His delusion is often short-lived.

Additionally, we are hardwired to be jealous, and if a partner is suddenly smitten with a new guy, spends time with him traditionally reserved for the couple, buys him flowers, and has great sex with him, the partner left out in the cold in the triad will be jealous. Stewart may enjoy having two men that he loves and even puffs out his chest with pride, but Joe and Evan, the two other gentlemen in his life, may have different thoughts and feelings especially when one or the other begins to take time away from the relationship with Stewart. Jealousy is no small issue, and we will explore it in the chapter on open relationships. For now, it suffices to recognize that jealousy in both the existing partner and the new third man in the relationship can and does appear.

The other obstacle to loving more than one person stems from passion. Recall that we tend to idolize our beloved and place him on a pedestal far above other human beings. He is wonderful. He is perfect. His body is incredible. His penis makes me hard just thinking of it. The sex between us is better than I have ever had. All of these sentiments (and more) arise when a partnered man finds himself passionately in love with a third person. Unfortunately, the more we idolize our new partner, the more our "old" partners looks, well, "old" and unappealing. Our partner or spouse has no chance of standing up against our beloved; he will always look the worse for the comparison. Chuck and Mike, for example, have been partners for four years and lived together for three of them. For the two of them, the honeymoon ended quite a while ago. Chuck, in particular, dropped his gym membership soon after moving in with Mike and went on to gain twenty-five obvious pounds. They know what they look like in a great number of unflattering situations, including sitting on the toilet, walking around on a Saturday morning in ratty underwear, unshaved, and sleeping on the sofa with a mouth wide open. When Mike meets Raymond while volunteering at a pride festival, they immediately hit it off. After several dinner dates, both are soon smitten with each other. Both Mike and Raymond increase the number of times they work out each week so as to be unashamed to undress in front of each other; they always dress their best (down to the sexiest underwear they dare try—no ratty drawers for these men); their time together is filled with meaningful discourses on each other's dreams and aspirations (no talk here of the banal necessities of daily life such as bills and the best food for the cat); and each night, knowingly stolen away from time with another man, is filled with dancing, the theater, or passionate sex with scented candles by the bedside. No, you won't find Mike and Raymond watching television with a beer in hand unable to muster the effort to engage in dialogue. Everything is so smooth, so effortless, and just so perfect between the two of them. How could Chuck ever hope to compete? Even minus the extra poundage and with the addition of new drawers, Mike cannot help but contrast the mundane life he lives with Chuck to the splendor of his discreet hours with Raymond. It's tough then to maintain an affair when one person appears hopelessly inept and unattractive in the unflattering shadow of a competing lover.

Given time, almost all affairs will begin to lose their magical aura, and the two involved men will begin to see the real person beneath the manipulated impression. As with any romantic relationship, the passion will fade, leaving two human beings naked of the aura of perfection that enveloped them during the early heights of the relationship. Even the most overwhelming and passionate of affairs crashes at some point. And at that point, the betraying spouse wakes as if from an enchanted state to ask, "What the hell was I thinking?" or—and this is less likely but it does happen—realizes that he really does love the new man, warts and all.

IN SUMMARY, even two men who love each other and have established a satisfying shared life together are just as likely to experience issues with nonmonogamy as the couple who have fallen out of love but remain together for convenience. Yes, even those satisfied with their relationship will still cheat. Some men may get away with infidelity, but for repeated infidelities and outright affairs, the subterfuge eventually implodes. A partner discovers his mate's sexual secrets, and, quite often, all hell breaks loose. This is the topic of the next chapter.

CHAPTER 7

Discovery of the Affair and What to Do about It

THIS CHAPTER IS WRITTEN for a couple coping with infidelity, whether this occurs within the parameters of an open relationship in which the sexual agreement has been broken or within a relationship in which monogamy was promised or assumed. Infidelity can be a one-time occurrence, a series of short-term sexual escapades with anonymous men, an afternoon of remembrance sex with a former lover, the presence of a fuck buddy of several months' to years' duration, or an actual affair as we typically picture it, including emotional and sexual gratification.

Discovery

A 1997 study asked men and women to list cues that might signify that their partner was sexually unfaithful. Other than the obvious one of actually stumbling upon a partner involved in a sexual act with another person, most of the cues were subtle:

- *Changes in a partner's sexual interest, particularly during*

sex when the partner is mechanical, uninterested, or has difficulty with sexual arousal
- *A sudden increase in sexual interest, including trying out new positions*
- *Changes in daily routine*

And if a partner had actually become involved emotionally *and* sexually with another person, other cues were assumed, including:

- *Ceasing to say "I love you"*
- *Emotional disengagement*
- *Failure to look one in the eyes*
- *Avoiding talking about a specific person in the third person*
- *Becoming nervous when the third person's name comes up in conversation*

Other indicators may be even more subtle, including less touching, more silence, less face-to-face conversation, and an indifferent or even cold vocal tone. Distancing too is common as evidenced by a decrease in the amount of time spent together, the amount of time spent talking to each other, and the presence of secrecy. Other than for infrequent one-night stands, I have yet to talk to a professional or couple who did not indicate that discovering partners sense some change in the dynamics of the relationship. This of course leads to repeated queries as to whether something is wrong or if the partner has become involved with somebody new. For the man who recognizes that something is amiss in the relationship but receives denials or excuses for the change from his partner (e.g., "Work is killing me right now"), the predicament is maddening, particularly when all he has to go on is a nebulous belief that something is not quite the same.

The actual detection of infidelity can occur in an endless number of ways. A friend may tell of us of seeing our lover in a compromising situation. Snooping might leads us to a cache of torrid e-mails. An argument leads to an admission. Guilt may cause a partner to reveal his infidelity. However it is discovered, how should one respond upon learning that a partner has been unfaithful? Kick him out? Make ultimatums? Maintain an icy stance toward him for months? Infantilize the partner by demanding to know his whereabouts and the people he is with every hour of the day?

To cope successfully with infidelity, the following therapeutic suggestions have proven beneficial:

1. *Slow down so as not to make rash decisions.*
2. *Deal with the emotions.*
3. *Discover what motivated the activity.*

Slow Down

Regardless of the circumstances of infidelity, the best decision is not to decide anything in the present or the immediate future. Emotions will be strong on both sides; the betrayed man will likely be hurt and his partner ashamed, confused, and/or obstinate. Even if one man says that he has fallen completely in love with another person and doesn't know if the pre-existing relationship can or will last or even if he wants it to last, for both partners the best decision is still to do nothing. Remember that even the most blazing hot affair will eventually lose its heat.

One partner can certainly lay down demands and ultimatums. "You can never see him again." "The relationship between the two of you is over as of now." "No more stopping at the park after work." "We go the gym together from this point on."

While agreeing that a hasty decision made during a period of strong emotions is likely to be regretted in the future, therapists who work with couples disagree as to whether the sexual activity occurring outside the relationship must immediately stop. Both sides present legitimate arguments. On one hand, the work of a couple who want to stay together in spite of discovered nonmonogamy must focus their attention on their own needs. Outside relationships only detract from this work. After all, if the problem affecting a relationship is non-monogamy, then additional nonmonogamous excursions are certainly not going to help.

The other side counters that in certain scenarios, ending additional sexual involvements is difficult, if not impossible. Demanding a man end an affair with another man with whom he has established feelings of intimacy and passion will likely not work. Men in this predicament cannot simply toss off these feelings and push a lover out of mind; the desire is too strong. Men involved in compulsive sexual behaviors cannot stop, but demands that they do just that will compel them to find better methods of concealing their additional sexual outlets. Men who have been in one-night stands or a string of anonymous sexual adventures may accept an ultimatum, particularly if a partner threatens termination of a relationship in which they wish to remain. A truly contrite (or frightened) partner may stop immediately, but this does not necessarily predict long-term monogamous behavior.

Be cautious what is told to friends and family. We might want to rush into the arms of our best friends to seek solace and sympathy for our anger toward the discovered spouse. Be careful, though, for if we decide to work on the relationship, our support system may not be quite so willing to give up their antipathy toward our partner even when the relationship is healed and working well. In addition, the advice we receive is colored by each person's history and belief system; each person has an opinion and possibly even a personal experience with infidelity, but we should not assume that these opinions and experiences have much relevance to our own present dilemma.

Cope with Emotions

Read the literature, talk to a straight couple coping with infidelity, or peruse a magazine article written for women on the same topic, and you will without doubt encounter descriptions of unbearable pain, searing rage, obsession with the sexual activities engaged in between the spouse and the third person, disorienting confusion, and often a desire for retribution. Discovering partners are not only furious at their mate but also themselves, and they ask themselves how they could be so blind? Additionally, we hear over and over again emotions of shame, vulnerability, and insecurity about the relationship. "What does your action mean for our relationship?" "What does your action indicate about me? I'm no longer good enough for you?" Emotions vacillate quickly between hate and

a desperate need to be recognized and comforted by the discovered spouse.

One would think that gay men, knowing as they do the negative stereotypes of gay promiscuity, would at least be inocu-
lated against such strong reactions. But according to the professionals I spoke with, this is not the case. The discovery of
infidelity is painful no matter what one's orientation happens
to be. Even in an open relationship that condones additional
sexual relationships, breaking the pact can be devastating. Vic
and Jeff, for example, had an open relationship in which each
were allowed separate lovers as long as these liaisons did not affect their relationship. And to aid in their commitment to each
other, they took a weeklong vacation once or twice a year in
which it was agreed that, for those short durations, they would
only have intimate contact with each other. Two weeks of faithful sexual commitment each year didn't seem too demanding.
Still, Vic was hurt, then enraged, to learn that Jeff still crept off
to have a twenty-minute sexual contact with a poolside waiter
while on the last trip. Sadly, it was the last trip they took
together.

Infidelity leads us to question the overall trustworthiness of
a partner. We rightly ask, "If he could do this to me, can I ever
trust him again with regard to *anything*?" We may begin to
have doubts about every area of our shared existence. Can I
trust him to pay the bills on time? Can I trust him to pick up
the cat from the vet? Is he responsible enough to get all this
damn pornography out of sight before my sister comes for a
visit? Even if he had always been an exemplar in regards to responsibilities, the newly discovered infidelity causes us to question every taken-for-granted aspect of our shared lives. In addition, we begin to reexamine the past and add a pernicious

shading to memories of our lives together. Was he out fucking around with someone else that night he said he had to work late? Is the reason that he didn't leave his credit card statement out this month because of incriminating evidence in the purchases? Was that night he angrily told me he was too tired for sex really because he had already had a blowjob in the park before coming home? We create fantasies—often elaborate—with a core theme of betrayal for even the most trivial of activities.

The discovering male is left to wonder about how important he is now to his partner. Do I now hold a second-place position in his life or in our sex life? Even men in open relationships can experience this concern if they find that another man appears to be surpassing their importance in the eyes of their partners. A recognized division between primary and secondary lovers as is seen in many open relationships can become a source of pain for a man if his partner allows or appears to allow another man to assume the ostensibly already taken primary position.

Infidelity also hurts us on a much deeper and profound psychological level. Psychologists often classify discovered incidents of infidelity as an "attachment trauma," and trauma is indeed an accurate description of infidelity from the perspective of the betrayed partner. Attachment theory informs us that we are biologically hardwired to seek safe, dependable relationships throughout our lifetimes. Most work on attachment has focused on the relationship between parents and children, but there is recognition that the need for a safe and secure relationship is as necessary for adults as it is for children. For most adults, our figures of security and safety are often our romantic partners. We have all encountered a child who is incapable of being comforted, who wails and screams uncontrollably until his mother returns, even if she has only gone for fifteen minutes. In truth, the removal of this primary attachment figure is a profoundly terrifying loss for a child.

Adults, though they may not demonstrate the overt terror of a child, can still exhibit despair, clinginess, and a need for reassurance. The loss of trust in a person whom we assumed to be a steadfast figure of security for us—whether a parent or a partner—activates a primordial terror that often cannot be reasonably allayed. Betrayed partners are in the unfortunate position of recognizing that their mate is not only the source of their pain but also, if they want to maintain the relationship, the ultimate solution to the problem. No amount of reasoning or logic will dispel grief from a failed attachment, and coping with infidelity means coping with emotional trauma.

Finally, the other most common response to a broken relationship agreement is obsession. Therapists who work with couples in crisis following the acknowledgment of infidelity actually try to normalize obsession because it is such a common occurrence. Questions about the identity or identities of additional lovers and sex partners and the details of the sexual activity become endless ruminations for the partner experiencing the loss of trust. He shouldn't be surprised to stay up all night unable to dislodge these thoughts from his head. Additionally, repeated scathing attacks on the discovered male are also common. Statements such as "How could you do this to me?" and "You'll never know how much this hurt me" are wielded again and again to both express pain and anger as well as elicit shame in the partner.

The man who has broken the relationship agreement will be inundated with questions of the most detailed and particular nature. One gentleman I worked with became increasingly frazzled by his partner's questions. Where did he have sex with other men? Did they have a better body than him? Did he give them oral sex (something he hadn't done with his partner for years)? Were his orgasms better with his anonymous contacts than with him? My client began to think that possibly his lover was experiencing some sort of vicarious thrill in learning all of these details. And unwisely he offered this interpretation to his partner. There are indeed many open relationships that thrive sexually on mutual recounting of outside sexual activities, but a partner who has discovered that his trusted mate has been sexually unfaithful is not looking for a vicarious thrill. My client's action did nothing to help the predicament, but he did indeed make things much worse.

While it is true that time heals all wounds, if months have gone by and emotions and obsession have not somewhat abated or have even gotten worse, it is definitely time for some professional intervention. Getting stuck in rage and obsession does not bode well for the life of the relationship. However, it is not up to the discovered partner to say, "Don't you think that it's time to get over this?" or "Haven't we gone over the details a thousand times already?" Instead this will only fan the flames. If pain and obsession do not decrease, if suicidal thoughts become evident, or if the idea of revenge is increasingly tempting, seek help. A therapist can provide structure for emotions and make sure that they don't lead to self-harm.

Getting through the initial shock and subsequent anger and obsession are essential for the survival of the relationship. But people do get stuck; their reactions—if continued for months on end without containment and concurrent therapeutic work—will add more toxins to a damaged relationship. It could well lead the discovered partner to actually leave when this is exactly just what the discovering spouse doesn't want to happen.

Information Gathering

It is very easy and tempting to slide into black-and-white thinking when infidelity is discovered. The discovering partner, friends, and family can all too easily label the discovered man guilty and deserving of punishment. Often however, simplistic notions of right and wrong evolve into complex accounts of the ongoing dynamics of a relationship. In his research on gay monogamy, Michael LaSala finds that couples who engage in outside sex while in a purportedly monogamous relationship have lower relationship quality and satisfaction than those in strictly monogamous or open relationships. On the other hand, the explanation for a sexual assignation could actually be quite uncomplicated: the opportunity simply arose and a man took advantage of it. In these cases, the activity does not reflect a systemic problem within the long-term relationship. In contrasting the differences between the Western perspective on infidelity and that of much of the rest of the world, Pamela Druckerman found that "outside America, they tend to accept that it's normal for married people to have little crushes and attractions, and to sometimes act on these feelings. When they do, it doesn't automatically mean that the married couple has been, in the American parlance, living a lie for years" (2007, p. 276).

When the presence of infidelity takes the foreground in a relationship, relevant factors need to be considered in guiding the couple on how to proceed. Just consider the following questions:

Did the discovered man have a single one-night stand?

*Have there been frequent episodes of infidelity with many
    other men?*

Is he passionately in love with another person?

*Has he had a longstanding hidden romantic relationship with
    another man for years?*

*How was the infidelity discovered? Did he come clean and on
    his own? Did his partner hear it from a friend or discover
    irrefutable evidence?*

*Was an affair or infidelity repeatedly denied, only for the
    truth to come out months later?*

Is the activity over, or is he still involved?

Did he have safe sex with the other individuals?

*Does he want to stop? Can he stop? Does he even have control
    over his behavior?*

*Is the discovery a complete surprise or more or less expected,
    though nonetheless unwanted?*

How faithful has the betrayed spouse been?

*Is the relationship a fairly satisfying one? Are there
    longstanding issues that have never been dealt with?*

*Is monogamy an agreed-upon expectation, or was this taken
    for granted by one person?*

*Do both partners want the relationship to last, or have there
    been doubts about its stability all along?*

When a discovered partner or spouse attempts to account
for an accusation of infidelity, it typically takes one of four
forms (Fitness 2001). The first is outright denial of any form of
infidelity. Such denial can happen repeatedly, with one man
certain that his partner is somehow not living up to the relationship agreement. If a man is engaged in a hidden affair with

another or is involved in repeated incidents of sexual activity, we already know that its effects leak into the primary relationship.

The second response to "are you having sex with another person" is an admission of guilt but in which the act and its seriousness are minimized. It didn't mean anything. It was *only* a one-night stand, and I'll never see this man again ever. I *just* needed something new; you're still the one that I love. Notice the use of qualifiers here such as "just" and "only," and such minimization adds insult to an already hurtful situation. Let us not forget that even if the male in question had a several-minute-long mutual masturbation encounter with a man in the sauna as his one sexual digression, for the discovering male who expected and believed in strict monogamy, the hurt and pain are exceedingly real.

The third response to confrontation over sexual activity outside of the relationship is admission of culpability along with extenuating circumstances. "I was drunk." "You haven't had sex with me in weeks." "We've been together for years; I just wanted to sample something new." "You're not interested in sex anymore, so what the hell was I supposed to do?" "I was so stressed out from work and from my father's illness that I didn't know what I was doing." Extenuating circumstances often take aim at dissatisfaction in the current relationship. As this book has already indicated, any of these can indeed be true. But they can also be used as a cover for a man to hide his own sexual compulsivity or deeper relationship concerns.

Landers and Mainzer (2005) make a salient point regarding extenuating circumstances: "The road to being the . . . cheater starts with manufactured complexity." Many men attempt to excuse their behavior by claiming, "It's too complicated. You wouldn't understand." They attempt to reconstruct the circumstances so that it appears they are the ones that have been suffering. And while this may be true, it could also be far less complicated. We already know that many happy men in happy relationships find themselves involved with extra-relational sex. The veneer of suffering and struggle that a man may offer as an excuse may indeed be just that: an excuse. If a spouse claims that the reason for sexual activity outside of the relationship is just too complicated or complex to put into words, it's a safe bet that this is an excuse with minimal legitimacy.

Finally, the last response to a question of infidelity has been found to be the most meaningful: a concession of the offense with a display of remorse and an attempt to improve the relationship. Remorse is particularly important if the discovered partner has been denying the existence of an extra-relational involvement for some time, making his partner question his own sanity.

Admission, Apology, and Remorse

Assuming that both men in the couple want to maintain their relationship, the best intervention is for the discovered spouse to admit to what he did and to apologize for the hurt he caused. Admission and apology do not include offering excuses, justifications, minimizing the behavior, and blaming the partner. Remorse, recognizing the pain and hurt experienced by the other person, is likewise essential. To simply apologize for the additional activity outside of the relationship without an acknowledgment of its influence on the other man rings hollow. Too many men are willing to offer instant apologies without trying to comprehend the pain they have caused their partners. Indeed, they may apologize repeatedly without once ever trying to understand the meaning and ramifications of their actions on their relationship.

Dr. Brian Case created a list of necessary steps in the admission process that he titled "The Process of Apology." His six steps contain, in one form or fashion, the myriad recommendations and suggestions of innumerable professionals with regard to the admission and apology process. These steps are directed at the discovered male:

1. *Acknowledge that the hidden sexual activity outside of the relationship was hurtful to the partner and the relationship as a whole.*

2. *Learn how the activity affected the partner and express an understanding of the impact. The discovered male often neglects to ask how the partner has been affected. Of course it's easier to elide or ignore this emotional factor, but apology can't work without it. A man presumes that he can imagine his partner's pain, but what he imagines may be inaccurate or a complete underestimation. The best thing is to ask how his actions have affected his partner.*

3. *Make restitution where needed and possible. It is incumbent on the partner to do as much as possible to reestablish trust. Restitution does not mean buying expensive gifts as a means of placating the hurt spouse but rather acting in ways that evidence a sincere effort at relationship-building. Mitch, for example, was not willing to forgo working out even though the gym was the very place he often met men for quick anonymous sexual interludes. Since his partner was not willing to join the gym for workouts even*

after Mitch's infidelity was discovered, Mitch bought a home gym and canceled his gym membership. Mitch hated working out at home, but his willingness to accept a secondary method of exercise that removed him from other available men was seen as a sign of goodwill.

4. *Learn how and why you did what you did, and share this understanding with your partner. This book has already touched upon problematic relationship patterns and infidelity.*

5. *Create a plan of action, share this with your partner, and follow through on it. For the couple who intend to live with an agreement of strict monogamy, this means creating a plan that will minimize relapse. This can include therapy to work on relationship issues, professional intervention to work on personal psychological and emotional issues, evaluation of high-risk situations, plans for avoidance of these situations, and possibly even some type of ceremony or written agreement signifying monogamy.*

6. *Overtly apologize and ask for forgiveness.*

Forgiveness

The discovering partner is not a passive person in the admission process sitting off to the side simmering in his tumult of emotions. He himself has work to do as well. First, he risks getting caught in obsession, rage, and a desire for retribution that can last for years and years. Of no less importance, a partner's infidelity could be an indication of ongoing relationship issues, and both partners therefore may have to engage in some work on themselves and on their relationship.

So what is the role of the discovering spouse in the admission process? According to the experts, the two goals are to cope with emotions and begin to rebuild the relationship. Emily Brown, a recognized expert in treatment of infidelity, offered a list of obstacles that hinder the discovering spouse from completing these two tasks, including:

- *Persistence of obsession*
- *Attempts to resolve the problem by making premature decisions*
- *Avoidance of underlying issues*
- *Blaming the infidelity on the partner and refusing to consider his own possible role in the infidelity*

Dr. Brian Case, not satisfied with formulating the steps necessary for the discovered spouse, also created a process of forgiveness for the discovering spouse. Note the word "process" here; forgiveness is not a one-time event but an ongoing series of steps. Case reminds us that once the torrent of emotion and pain in the early period of discovery has passed and the discoverer has opted for forgiveness and the rebuilding of relationship trust, his job is to get in touch with his own feelings of hurt and anger, express them in non-hurtful ways, consider if he himself somehow played a role in the infidelity, and make proactive changes to reestablish a trusting relationship.

Post-Relationship Implications

Even for the most committed couple intent on reestablishing trust, the process of admission and forgiveness do not end the repercussions of infidelity, for there is no magical threshold a couple can cross in which all of the negative feelings cease to exist. Infidelity is a trauma for many couples, and its echoes, though far less overpowering than in the early stages of discovery, still resound months and even years later. Don-David Lusterman cautions that time does not necessarily heal all wounds and that discovered infidelity can lead to Post-Traumatic Stress Disorder. Small, seemingly minute details can set off an emotional reaction long after infidelity has been processed. The cloud of infidelity that hovers over many a relationship does not disappear overnight; sometimes, perpetual insecurity about the relationship is an outcome.

The discovering spouse may need more reassurance than he needed before the infidelity was discovered. The discovered spouse may need to account for his behaviors and whereabouts so as to assuage his partner's doubts. Dan, for example, has called Vaughn twice a day from his office for years to verify his location. God help the man who comes home an hour later than he said he would after infidelity had been discovered. As a tangent to this, the discovering spouse may try to control his partner. Check-in times may be demanded, and friends and recreational venues may need to be scrutinized. Small incidents such as seeing a film that depicts infidelity or learning of a friend's problems with the same issue can cause the couple to revert back to working on trust.

Friends and family, the same people that the discovering spouse turned to in his emotional turmoil, may not be so willing to forgive the discovered spouse. Even if the relationship is doing better than before the infidelity was discovered may not suffice as evidence for the forgiveness of friends and family.

Ultimately, no amount of oversight can protect a couple

from infidelity. The process of admission, apology, and forgiveness is meant to reestablish trust, and thus we must trust our partner at some point. The reality is that we cannot prevent infidelity from happening even in couples who have already experienced it and worked through the apology and forgiveness process. Discovered infidelity can even be an impetus for two men to consider other sexual configurations.

Three Destinations

In spite of the seeming chaos that can envelop the couple, there are really only three roads that the relationship can enter upon when infidelity is discovered, each with its own clear destination. First, is the ending of the relationship. And while it might be easy to say "Toss the lout out," let us not forget all of the information presented earlier in this book. Finding another man who can maintain long-term monogamy after passion has subsided and who also meets the majority of other criteria that we want in a relationship further limits the already limited number of available men out there. And of course the dilemma here is that we don't find out if our new partner is capable of long-term monogamy (if that is what we want) until the long term. By the time we learn that he is just as handicapped in sexual exclusivity as our previous partners, we may have already invested years. Ending a relationship on good terms and avoiding or at least minimizing the drama that can occur at the end of a gay male relationship can actually pay healthy dividends in the future. Yes, revenge is sweet, but it can, and often does, come back to haunt us.

If our partner is a man whom we truly love and who has too

many good qualities to allow us to toss the relationship away, we may, instead of ending it, find a way to make it work. Of course in our rage, we may occasionally want to not only to end the relationship, all contact with him, and have occasional daydreams of homicide (this is not an exaggeration; it does happen), but if we are willing to mutually work together, we may find that infidelity really can lead to a stronger relationship. I recognize that the person who has just discovered that his partner or boyfriend was seen offering oral sex at the downtown all-male cinema does not want to hear this, but it is still true.

The second and third roads that a couple can enter upon lead to destinations of forgiveness, reconciliation, and stronger and more meaningful relationships. However, there is a slight difference in itineraries in how these destinations are reached, and the major difference is the requirement for monogamy. On this second road, forgiveness and reconciliation lead to a relationship in which men will try even harder to maintain sexual exclusivity. The couple again makes a commitment to live their sexual lives within the confines of their relationship.

In a 1998 interview for *The Advocate*, Deepak Chopra offered the following suggestion for those couples agreeing to enter upon this second path: "The confusion for many couples is that after they've been together for a while, they may feel the sexuality between them diminishes. They think something's wrong—especially gay couples. . . . Therefore, they might abandon the journey and start all over again with someone else. That's just a stage of immaturity. It doesn't matter if you're gay or straight. It's a statement of maturity to come to a place where you say 'I can't have everything all the time. In the end I have to settle for meaningfulness and fulfillment and love, which is must more than just sexuality.'"

Couples who recommit to monogamy understand that it takes much more than just a stupendous sex life to create a lasting successful relationship. This does not mean that the sex between them is unsatisfying or unpleasant, only that it is qualitatively different and less frequent than what occurred during the passionate early stage of the relationship. Those who seek this destination can skip the next chapter, which describes open relationships, and instead move on to Chapter Nine, an overview of the research on sexual enrichment.

One final caveat for couples trying once again to live monogamously: Sometimes both partners willingly agree that they should remain monogamous, but just as often one partner is more vociferous in this demand. Typically this is the discovering partner. The straying partner might acquiesce to this demand without comment since he is already in the doghouse and doesn't want to stir up any more negative emotion than he already has.

The third and final road also aims for forgiveness and reconciliation but with an understanding that monogamy probably isn't going to work in the long term. The couple who take this road negotiate a new form of relationship in which sexual exclusivity is not an expectation or a requirement. On this third road, the couple who already had an open relationship will redefine and commit to the rules for additional sexual outlets and relationships. These open relationships are seldom truly open to complete sexual freedom. Even the most open of relationships still sets some parameters. In this last journey the couple realizes that in spite of the infidelity, the relationship remains an important and desirable entity; both men want it to survive. This time, however, they accept the inevitability of waning passion and the desire for sexual novelty and try in their own way to somehow make the relationship work while recognizing these realities. The next chapter examines this decision.

There is one final route chosen by couples, but we do not include it as a viable option: purposeful ignorance. One man continues to engage in infidelity while the other pretends it isn't happening. The discovering partner continues to act as if the couple is monogamous while knowing that this really isn't true. Or to make matters even more complicated, both partners may engage in continued infidelity but still pretend to be monogamous. No questions are ever asked. As you can well imagine, such a relationship is rife with complications, and there is a professional consensus that this relationship is not a healthy one.

CHAPTER 8
Open Relationships

As Bob Dylan sang "The times they are a-changing." In the past fifty years we have opened ourselves to a wealth of new marital and family configurations. We can have straight, gay, or transgender marriages. We can have domestic partnerships. We can be single parents, stepparents, adoptive parents, or child-free. Successive marriages and blended families are common. We can cohabit and never marry, or we can be in a commuter marriage with only brief stints under one roof. Finely attuned to the fragility of matrimony, we now have prenuptial agreements and no-fault divorce. All these arrangements have redefined boundaries both within the couple and between the couple and the outside world. Yet, however elastic our attitudes toward marriage, we remain unflinching in our insistence on monogamy. With few exceptions—move stars, aging hippies, swingers—the borders we draw around sexual exclusivity remain rigid.—Esther Perel, *Mating in Captivity* (p. 177)

Let me say this up front. I have numerous friends in open relationships. That said, only a few of them have managed to turn this type of arrangement into something that strikes me as loving and functional. Meaning, they have stayed together

for longer than a few weeks and haven't ended the relationship by hurling beer bottles at one another outside of a West
Hollywood nightclub because one of them slept with a mutual friend who was deemed off-limits.—Christopher Rice,
The Advocate, 2005

It has been noted . . . that some extrarelationship sex, whether
comfortable or not, seems to be the norm for established male
couples . . . this behavior may represent a healthy adaptation
for some couples. But these arrangements may also signal separation and attachment difficulties . . . [This] may be an individual's way of announcing his anxieties and fears about being in an intimate relationship.—Eli Coleman and Rex Reece,
1988

Though there are many variations in the ground rules for sexual activity in relationships, they are all still variations of just a
few core themes. A couple may opt for mutual celibacy, to remain monogamous for the duration of the relationship, choose
some form of open relationship, or have occasional or even frequent covert sexual activity outside the parameters of their established relationship. None of these decisions is written in
stone, and they can and often do change, particularly in an environment that places so much importance on sexual satisfaction. Two men might start out very much desiring sexual exclusivity; nonmonogamy is simply not an option. As the years
go by though, one or both partners may want to modify this
initial agreement to allow at least occasional additional sexual
partners or to permit a threesome when the opportunity arises.
Other couples may start out with very open relationships in
which each man is allowed to engage in as much sexual activity

as he desires outside their pairing. But as these two men grow older, they may decide to place limits on this additional sexual activity or even choose monogamy. A couple could experience several transitions during their time together, from monogamy to open relationships and back to monogamy. They may even start as a couple, form a romantic threesome for months to years, and then revert back to a couple. And throughout the years, there might be an occasional hidden sexual dalliance.

One professional I interviewed, the clinical director of a facility that offered counseling for gay and lesbian couples, laughed when I told him that I was writing a chapter on open relationships for gay male couples. "Why write about the obvious?" he said. Over and over again I either read or heard similar responses. One e-mail I sent out to recognized professionals who work with gay men asked "can open relationships work?" One terse response was, "What century are you living in? Is this the 1960s or the 21st century?" It seems axiomatic that gay men can (and according to many *should*) be engaged in open relationships. Adherents and supporters of the different variations of open relationships point out that we don't want to ape the reigning heterosexual model. Additionally, monogamous relationships were more feasible when the human lifespan was much shorter and a relationship might end with death after twenty or so years; but is it possible to remain both romantically and sexually involved with the same person for fifty years? How are we expected to maintain sexual excitement with the same person when brain science indicates that our sexual passion for one person begins to dampen after approximately seventeen months and that romantic relationships around the world tend to end at the four-year mark?

The most vocal supporters of open relationships claim that

they offer a formula for healthy autonomy, that they do not require partners to subordinate their needs and interest, and that they create ever-expanding meaningful gay communities through the multitude of connections that form. Open relationships are seen by many who practice them as harbingers of relationship patterns that will someday become the norm. One presenter at a workshop on gay male relationships proudly told the assembled audience that a century from now, historians will look back and see that gay men were the galvanizing force for sweeping societal changes in relationships. In his view (and one shared by many), we are all moving toward more open relationship configurations.

Probably the most vehemently outspoken critic of monogamy I have encountered is Edmund White, author of many fiction and nonfiction books on gay topics and a professor at Princeton University. In a 1998 article for *The Advocate*, he wrote, "I would argue that monogamy is part of a pleasure-hating package being sold by aging gay leaders, now in their 50s and 60s, people who through some ghastly process of natural selection managed to survive the plague [AIDS] precisely because they were so dysfunctional that they could never get laid. . . . The virus selected against men who were affectionate, progressive, and fun-loving and left us with these boring old prudes." In his ideal perspective, "Promiscuity, no matter how much fun, never replaced the need for intimacy, but we felt that closeness could come in many forms and that it could be experienced with several people. No longer would we subscribe to the unworkable model of marriage. Now we'd buy a house or start a business with a compatible partner, who might call forth our deepest sense of commitment. But we'd also have extracurricular sex, either with regular sex buddies, who might or might not be friends, or with a succession of strangers, met at the baths or on the street."

I contacted Mr. White to see if he has tempered these views in the passing of the decade since he wrote these statements. "My own feeling is that with my partner of twelve years we have so much esteem for one another that we want each other to be happy—even if that means happy (temporarily) with someone else," he replied. "The dominant metaphor in male gay relationships is 'the best friend'—and don't we always want the most and the best for our friends?"

White complained that gay men were now so busy seeking to replicate middle-class values (i.e., monogamous relationships and their acceptance by the church) that they have forgotten their role as vanguards in battling political, social, and religious injustice and oppression. Eminent researcher of gay relationships Michael LaSala has a similar perspective: "Monogamy is a societal norm that frankly hasn't worked well for many straights. Sadly, in the rush to get married, I think many gay men have also embraced some of marriage's most repressive aspects, including sexual monogamy."

While some therapists and writers (including myself) have noted the growing prevalance of gay monogamy, open relationships still flourish. For example, it is not an overstatement to say that there is practically no book on gay relationships, whether written for the popular press or for the professional audience, which does not mention the topic of open relationships. As research, I examined relationship self-help books written for gay couples published in the past decade. Not surprisingly, every one discussed open relationships. But surprisingly, in light of the often-vocal approbation of open male relationships—not only can we be in open relationships, but we *should* be in open relationships—these books were much more reserved in their advice. I did not find exhortations to change monogamous relationship configurations or even an open embrace of open relationships. Instead, these books were either neutral in their tone or disapproving of the entire concept.

Michael Kantor, a psychiatrist who specializes in gay male issues and the author of *My Guy* and *Together Forever: The Gay Man's Guide to Lifelong Love* was the most vociferously disapproving of open relationships. Open relationships, he wrote, will be "encumbered by a heavy satchel of hurt feelings, personal guilt, and fear of recrimination, retribution, and retaliation—a harsh burden to bear while traversing what was supposed to be a road that led only to happiness." Dr. Richard Isay, author of numerous books on gay male psychological development and past chairman of the Committee on Gay and Lesbian Issues of the American Psychiatric Association, finds that within two to three years the sexually exclusive male couple begins to looks for sexual gratification outside of the primary relationship, and within five years, almost all male couples are no longer sexually exclusive. His primary concern is that "sex with strangers and the adventures that accompany it are so compelling and exciting that sooner or later, random sexual contacts subvert desire for a more familiar pattern." In other words, sexual arousal with another person is so stimulating, so exciting, and so rewarding (recall the dopamine system in the brain that is activated by both sexual arousal and drug use) that familiar sex with our partner, even though loving and comfortable, cannot compare. Our primary relationship suffers when we opt for some form of open relationship. My clinical experience incidentally concords with Dr. Isay; anonymous sexual encounters offer such stimulation that primary partners become "vanilla" and bland.

Other authors take a more neutral stance. In their respective texts, Dr. Betty Berzon, Dr. Kenneth George, and Jeffrey Chernin all state that open relationships can work but that an explicit understanding of the parameters must be mutually agreed to by both partners. Open relationships, they agree, take as much work as a monogamous relationship, and sometimes more. So to answer my own originating question, of course open relationships can work. But just as surely, they will not work for all couples. Many couples most certainly won't even consider this as an option. And in spite of the seeming ubiquitous praise heaped upon gay male open relationships, they can take just as much effort as traditional forms and, in addition, offer a host of other issues and problems that these latter couples won't have to face. Choosing an open relationship should be a careful decision that weighs all the potential advantages and disadvantages.

Types of Open Relationships

People mean different things by the term "open relationship." It would be helpful to have a better understanding of the more common relationship forms that are often defined as open relationships. Note that these are not just circumscribed to gay men; all couples, regardless of orientation, can choose one or more of these relationships:

Swingers—This term sounds so outdated, so 1960s and 1970s. Still, most people understand what kind of relationship configuration the term denotes. Couples who participate in this activity share partners or participate as partners in group sexual activities. Swinging is based almost completely on sex; there is no attempt to form permanent partnerships with another person or a couple. Of course, two couples could find that they really enjoy their mutually shared activity and become exclusive with one another.

Open Relationships/Open Marriages—An open relationship differs from swinging in that committed partners are allowed to engage in additional sexual contact outside of their primary relationship without the other partner being present. Toby and Raphael, for example, agree that each is allowed to have as much as sex outside the relationship as they can, as long as no emotional attachment occurs with a sex partner, the activity is kept outside of their household (e.g., no bringing men home, no phone calls from sex partners to and from the house) and all sex is performed safely (e.g., no anal sex). Both men also agree to share details of their additional sexual involvements with each other. As stated earlier, open relationships are rarely completely open in that each partner is allowed unfettered sex with outside men. The couple make rules for the activity and hopefully revisit them on a not-too-infrequent basis. It is important to note that issues of trust can be just as pertinent for open relationships as for monogamous ones. Studies find that there are perceived benefits and drawbacks to open relationships. Advantages include increased communication between partners, enhanced personal fulfillment, and increased sexual satisfaction. Disadvantages include jealousy, possessiveness, and problems arising due to issues

of time allotment between the two men in the primary re-
lationship and additional sex partners.

Polyamorous Relationships—"Polyamory" is defined as sexual
and emotional involvement with more than one partner.
Typically this takes three forms. First, one or both men in
the couple may have an ongoing secondary relationship;
there is no attempt to hide this, otherwise the presence of se-
crecy would define this as an affair. Second, a man has two
or more ongoing consistent relationships with lovers in
which there is minimal commitment to each. There is no
primary relationship, and this configuration can be thought
of as living a single life but having several simultaneous
lovers. Third, three or more men share a primary relation-
ship. A 2006 Advocate *story titled "Big Gay Love" asked the*
question "Does gay polygamy work?" The article intro-
duced several polyamorous male couples and discussed the
joys and tribulations inherent in their relationships. Dale
and Chaz, for example, had been a couple for five years
who would occasionally find a third person to "spice up"
their sex life. They had no intention of inviting any of these
men into their lives on a permanent or even semi-perma-
nent basis. One evening they met John at a restaurant, and
"all the rules went out the window because it felt so right."
They reported being committed to one another, including
exchanging rings and celebrating an anniversary. All the
"couples" in the article owned property together, shared
their finances, and had power of attorney for one another.

In the same article, Michael Bertolucci, a marriage and family therapist in West Hollywood, stated that these types of rela-

tionships have their positives and negatives. "What I tell my clients is, 'You know how hard it is to have a relationship with two people," he said. "Now magnify that." Some of the challenges mentioned by the interviewed men included disapproval by friends and, most often, family, and a need for increased communication and reflection about relationship dynamics. None of the polyamorous couples interviewed for the *Advocate* article expected legal recognition of their unions. And as for some type of church recognition . . . forget it. "The distinguishing feature of Christian marriage is, for many, a strict sexual exclusivity between two and only two partners—at least according to the ideal . . . If straight couples have to pay the price of sexual exclusivity in order to get married . . . shouldn't gay couples have to pay too? . . . We'll let you in, but only to the strictest, most old-fashioned model of marriage" (Jordan 2005, pp. 157–158).

The Ups and Downs of Open Relationships

What is clear at this point is that open relationships offer both advantages and disadvantages. They require just as much trust as a monogamous relationship, present with their own set of complexities, and do not completely circumnavigate infidelity. Yet they can work if planned carefully. Consider the following two accounts:

Marcus and Paulo have been a couple for ten years. Throughout this time, Paulo has suffered from periods of severe depression that have twice required hospitalization and for much of their time together, Marcus was often a caretaker, support person, and cheerleader for his partner. After numerous trials with pharmacological agents, Paulo found near-miraculous success with a new antidepressant. He is no longer depressed, is able to function at his job, and is actually finding satisfaction in his life. Unfortunately, the most common unwanted side effect of this new drug is a loss of libido. Paulo simply has loss interest in sex, and when sexual activity does occur, he cannot ejaculate (a common side-effect with SSRI anti-depressants). Paulo does not wish to begin examining substitute drugs as this could risk a return to his godawful depression. After careful consideration, he chooses to remain on his current prescription.

Marcus supports Paulo's decision but is himself not ready to forego sexual activity for the remainder of his life. He had already accepted a reduction of sexual activity in his life during Paulo's depressed period but is unwilling to accept masturbation or sex with his uninterested partner for too long. Thus the two men agreed to meet with a counselor experienced with open relationships to discuss options and a protocol. Neither of the men was interested in bringing a new man into their relationship and instead decided that Marcus could engage in additional sexual activity outside of the relationship. Issues such as information sharing, parameters for sexual activity outside of the relationship, assuring primacy of their relationship over all other involvements, teaching pre-emptive interventions for jealousy, and decisions as to who in their circle of friends and family need to know this arrangement were all mutually decided.

As per their agreement, Marcus shared the details of his sexual flings with Paulo. The latter's reactions were discussed each time, and the two men continued to see their therapist both as a couple and on an individual basis intermittently to ascertain if the agreement was having a negative effect on their relationship. Twice in the past year, Paulo requested that Marcus bring home another man for them to share. Though Paulo was unable to ejaculate during their time together, he did use the episode later for fantasy. At their last session with the therapist, both men agreed that an open relationship had increased their relationship satisfaction, their communication, and their trust and openness.

Our second couple, consisting of George and Adam, also began an open relationship. George works as an administrator for a large health care provider and brings home a large salary; Adam, in contrast, works in a small card store and earns an hourly rate commensurate with this type of service position. The couple takes two vacations per year and visits nearby New York City for a weekend of Broadway at least once every two months. George, of course, is the man who pays for these trips, though Adam does save up some of his small salary to at least pay some of the expenses. George has become increasingly bored in his sexual relations with Adam after six years as a couple. He is far more impulsive and demanding in his life, including his sexual desires; in fact, both men recognize that George has a far stronger sex drive than Adam.

George has recently become enamored with Internet pornography, but still he realizes an aching need inside for additional sexual liaisons that no amount of masturbatory fantasy can assuage. Being a forthright person (often labeled "brutally honest" in his job evaluations), he broaches the topic of open relationships with Adam. Not surprisingly Adam is not overjoyed with the prospect but reluctantly agrees after cajoling and imploring by George. Over the first few months, Adam makes no effort to engage in additional sexual activity outside of the relationship. He is not sure what George is doing, as no mention is made of any liaisons. Adam has noted, however, that George does receive more phone calls than usual that he takes in the privacy of his study. In addition, the sex between them, once infrequent, is now nonexistent. Adam wants to ask questions. Indeed, he has many. But he is reluctant to bring them up because he did agree to the open relationship. He is also beginning to fear for the sanctity of their relationship.

In the above two scenarios, we see some of the issues that can present in open relationships. The first couple, Marcus and Paulo, approach the idea cautiously and come to a mutual decision about the guidelines and practicalities that will apply. Of no less importance, each man continues to actively investigate how an open relationship affects them as a couple. An open relationship is a work in progress that requires continual re-reevaluation and modification. Two men do not need to obtain the services of a therapist to assist in structuring an open relationship, but they do need to be as painstakingly detailed as this couple were in planning and monitoring their arrangement. Jumping headfirst into an open relationship without planning and honest communication is a setup for future mishap.

The second couple, George and Adam, are far more typical of how a male couple approach an open relationship. They do indeed jump in headfirst with little planning and foresight of how this decision can affect their already established relationship. In their scenario, it is obvious that Adam is reluctant to allow this to occur but obliges anyway. We can conjecture that there are a multitude of issues already present in this relationship; sexual boredom is just one of many, and therapists would likely begin an exploration at the level of power differential between the two men. Michael Bertolucci, the therapist interviewed for the earlier *Advocate* article on polyamorous relationships, stated that in his experience many men turn to such arrangements because they are not having their needs met in a committed relationship with just one other person. The general professional consensus is that a relationship rife with issues and complications will not survive as an open relationship. The reality is that maintaining a successful open relationship requires a strong foundation between the two primary men. Ignored issues will not disappear because a third person has joined our life or because we can now have sex with a new person whenever we so desire. Thus before a couple seriously contemplates any form of open relationship, an honest and mutual appraisal of the health, stability, and cohesiveness of their already existing relationship must occur. Serious issues that have been ignored or relegated to silence need to be aired.

Finally, and of great importance, the decision must be mutual; this is not always the case. As therapist Michael Bettinger informed me, the men in the couple will either come to a resolution or an impasse. It is up to them to work it out. Mutually. And what if the impasse cannot be bridged? Three options remain. The relationship will end, the partner more desirous of nonmonogamy will have to learn to satisfy his needs within the parameters of the relationship, or he will cheat.

The Ground Rules for Open Relationships

In an interview for *The Advocate* in 1998, author and spiritual guru Deepak Chopra was asked about monogamy and open relationships. He supported both but was careful to advise, "Intimacy in a relationship requires that there are no hidden agendas. I think as long as the relationship is a complete and total communication of what the expectations are, then the relationship will be fulfilled." For those couples in which there is a more-or-less equal balance of power and in which relevant relationship issues have been addressed, the possibility exists that a long-term and nonmonogamous relationship can be maintained, provided some ground rules are followed, including:

Limits of sexual behavior—What does sexual activity with a third person encompass? This can range from self-masturbation while watching another male do the same to mutual masturbation to oral sex to penetrative sex. Couples may agree to a third person only as long as it becomes a threesome of which both partake. Couples talk about whether a third person must be anonymous or if friends (or even former lovers) are allowable. Even more, can a person engage in sexual activity with the same third party more than one time? This heightens risk to the couple as each additional contact may lead to an emotional attachment to the third person. It is imperative then for a couple considering nonmonogamy to define the limits of "sexual activity" for themselves. What are partners both allowed and not allowed to do with third persons? The couple must also monitor the effects of an open relationship on their own sexual interactions since sex with third parties can lead to a decrease in sexual activity within the primary relationship. If this is problematic or unacceptable to one or both partners, it is indeed time to reevaluate the relationship agreement.

Disclosure—Some couples make it a point to reveal to each other third-person sexual involvements. Others take the "don't ask, don't tell" approach. Finally, some couples use these incidents as fodder for their own sexual relations and stimulate one another to a tale of that afternoon's liaison in the bathroom of the local mall. An agreement as to the rules for disclosure is yet another essential for successful nonmonogamy. It seems that the most common approach is a sharing of details between partners.

Where or when—Are third-person sexual involvements allowable at any point of the year? Nonmonogamous couples may choose only to be so during certain stipulated time periods. One couple informed me that they were monogamous for fifty-one weeks of the year; they took off one week for third-person sexual activity when they attended a yearly clothing-optional gay men's retreat.

Continual renewal of the primary relationship—One of the most repeated concerns in the literature on open relationships is the desire for partners to remain "special" to each other. Thus many men have created their own classification system of primary and secondary relationships. An established long-term partner is the primary partner and others are secondary (except in the case of polyamorous relationships, in which case all the involved men are primary partners to one another). In an open relationship, both men must make proactive efforts to continually show that they value each other above other men in their lives. In terms used throughout this book, the primary relationship should have an emotional commitment not present in secondary relationships.

Professionals advise couples in open relationships to avoid outside sex when relationship problems are occurring. When a couple is experiencing stress, this is likely not the best time to seek the comfort and pleasure of an outside lover or sex partner. Instead this is the time to work on the primary relationship.

In his 2004 book *Keeping Mr. Right*, Kenneth George offered a sample agreement for an open relationship. Reminding us that such an agreement must be voluntary, mutual, workable, and acceptable to both men, he presented the following pact for a particular couple. This agreement won't work for all couples but is a starting point for exploration.

- *I will only engage in safer-sex behaviors.*
- *I will come home every night.*
- *I will not have sex with anyone else in our home.*
- *I will tell you about it.*
- *I will not get involved with anyone I have sex with, such as going out on a date, having dinner with him, going to a movie, etc.*
- *I will only engage in the following sexual behaviors:*
  Oral sex
  Masturbation
  Kissing
  Caressing

Jealousy

Jealousy is the most noted concern in open relationships and can and does occur in spite of even the most painstaking planning and preparation. In fact, in Michael LaSala's research on male couples, monogamous couples cite the avoidance of jealousy as a primary reason for choosing sexual exclusivity. Many of the disagreements and much of the anger in open relationships can be traced back to jealousy. Undue attention to a secondary lover can result in jealousy in a primary partnership; the reverse is also true. When a sex buddy or a secondary relationship begins to resent our attention to our primary lover, this could be evidence of jealousy. Douglas, for example, was increasingly incensed that he was unable to enjoy major holidays with his lover Sandy. Though Sandy had never lied and made it clear from the very beginning that he would spend holidays and vacation with his long-term partner Ishmael, Douglas was finding this agreement difficult to maintain after three years.

We now recognize that jealousy is hardwired into the human brain and is most likely to be primed in situations involving infidelity and perceived infidelity. The research base on jealousy is far too expansive to cover in this section, and it deserves a book on its own (for example Buss's *The Dangerous Passion: Why Jealousy Is as Necessary as Love and Sex*). In short, though, the role of jealousy is to motivate an individual to protect a mate from a rival, and, supportive of that description, a large literature base has formed on the concept of mate protection and jealousy. Buss reports that individuals may intentionally provoke a jealous reaction in their partner as a means to stave off an impending sexual transgression. When a man in a primary relationship believes that he is somehow losing his privileged position to another ostensibly secondary partner, jealousy and its behavioral manifestations occur. Jealousy can masquerade as rage, as increased efforts to engage the sexual interest of other people, and less obviously, self-abasement and submission. If a man is afraid that he is losing his partner, one strategy is to try even harder to please him.

Once a man believes he is no longer any more important than his mate's other sexual partners, problems arise. Just telling a partner that he is more special than all other lovers is not sufficient. Indications of this privileged position include spending more time together than with other men, celebrating specific holidays together, taking vacations together, and engaging in sexual acts that are not permissible with secondary relationships.

Sometimes the established rules for disclosure clash with the need to maintain a primary partner at his privileged primary relationship status. Coming home to tell a partner that one has had the very best sex in one's life with a stranger is certain to be painful news for him. Likewise acknowledging an infatuation with a new man can be hurtful (as well as threatening). Discretion is essential, particularly in sharing details that might undermine a partner's sense of specialness as well as suppressing any indications of enthusiasm or passion for the third person.

In his research, Michael LaSala found that a threesome in which both men in a couple have sex with the same outside partner is the least likely scenario to elicit jealousy. Additionally, in comparison to nonmonogamous couples who did not limit themselves to threesomes, these men reported a far more positive impact of outside sex on their relationships.

Disapproval

Open relationships risk the disapproval of friends, family, and the occasional consternation of neighbors. To many in the general public, these arrangements indicate an aberration of underlying pathology of the men involved, particularly that gay men have profligate and unmanageable sexual desires. Even other gay men offer tirades against open relationships. The societal expectation that a relationship between two people should be able fulfill all needs (including sexual) is still the rule of the land. Those who cannot meet their needs in a dyad of two people must accordingly have some pathology, most often informally diagnosed as a fear of intimacy. In addition, they are pejoratively labeled as selfish and self-serving. Finally, open relationships are seen as a corrupting influence on those men and women who attempt to maintain monogamy.

Many authors have noted the discrepancy between the American stance on infidelity and on divorce. Michele Scheinkman, for example, says, "It has always been interesting to me that American culture has great tolerance for divorce—where there is a total breakdown of the loyalty bond and painful effects for the whole family—but it is a culture with no tolerance for sexual infidelity." The same holds true for open relationships. We would rather see a couple break apart rather than find success with a new configuration. While I find that some open relationships are not as mutually beneficial as they appear on the surface—that quite often one partner has gone along without the enthusiasm of the other, that they are used to avoid relationship issues, and that the long-term stability of open relationships remains an unanswered question—those who do make it work are able to find great satisfaction in their lives.

CHAPTER 9
Sexual Enrichment

SINCE THIS IS A BOOK on monogamy, it is not surprising to find that much of its content has been on sex. Furthermore, readers can be forgiven for concluding that sexual satisfaction is the most important component of a successful relationship. This, however, is not true, and we all know that successful relationships require more than mutual sexual satisfaction. Indeed, the most successful relationships are repeatedly found to have excellent communication between partners. Research even finds that meaningful communication between partners compensates for a lack of sexual satisfaction. Thus it is not surprising that many interventions for relationship improvement begin at the levels of communication skills building. But in spite of the ascendance of communication, sexual satisfaction still ranks as very important for relationship success.

In gay self-help books there is a general lack of a meaningful response to queries such as: "Help, I'm just not sexually attracted to my partner any longer." How does a man—and his partner—deal with a lack of sexual desire? Gay men have been advised that while dating, if there is a lack of sexual spark after two or three dates, they are wasting their time. Move on to somebody else. But how does this apply to the long-term couple who see each other every night and for whom the sexual spark has already diminished if not completely died? Do we also just move on? This is an extremely important issue since all long-term couples will have to deal with waning passion and desire.

Interventions for problems with sexual desire presuppose a belief that by working on our relationship in general, we will simultaneously improve sexual dynamics. Supposedly, improvements in the former necessarily improve the latter. But our own sexual proclivities and desires occur at physiological and psychological levels too deep for general relationship interventions. There are profound undercurrents to our sexuality that cannot be altered. Our efforts at relationship improvement will move our sex lives in the right direction, but still, only so far.

Let's examine a common sexual issue: a discrepancy in sex drives between the two partners in a couple. Owen is far more focused on sex than his partner, Gary. For Gary, sex twice a month is more than sufficient. For Owen, however, sex several times a week is the preference. And as is very common for couples with this kind of libido difference, the issue is not directly addressed; both men believe that the other is not sensitive to his needs. Relationship-building skills will improve the abilities of these two men to communicate their sexual needs and wants and negotiate these differences. Simmering feelings of resentment may well decrease also. Therapy may also locate some of the underlying historical factors that led to each man's differences. What relationship building will not do, however, is markedly increase Gary's libido or decrease Owen's. We simply cannot be sure that sex will improve for these men when such a difference in sexual drive is evident. Sex and sexuality are not only affected by our upbringing, internal psychology, relationship dynamics, and physical health; it is also hardwired into our very being. Changing hardwired aspects of our being is often impossible.

It is the rare book that explicitly engages the reader in a comprehensive overview of the issue or gives explicit suggestion and directives for sexual improvement. Michael Kantor, in his usual blunt style, is such a rarity in that he offers the following advice for a bored couple: Engage in "no-holds-barred sex with him and him alone, and all the time . . . frequency and exclusivity is enough to wear out and cut through the sexual block." In other words, just keeping fucking away with our partner until sex improves. If only it were that easy . . .

Sexual Disorders

Therapeutic and clinical awareness of problematic sexual functioning in gay males is very recent. From a historical perspective, until 1973, when the American Psychological Association removed homosexuality from its manual of mental illnesses, most gay men entering therapy were seeking advice on how to change their orientation or how to adapt to a world that did not accept them. Gay men did not go to therapists to find methods of improving their sex lives. The removal of homosexuality from the category of mental illness allowed gay men to enter therapy to work on self-acceptance, to root out internalized homophobia, and to embrace their sexuality. Improved sex was still not a priority. Even the intervening AIDS epidemic, with its direct spotlight on sexual activity, offered little assistance for the myriad sexual issues not related to HIV that could still pose a challenge for couples. Gay men could recite verbatim the guidelines for safe sex but still had minimal knowledge of conditions such as erectile dysfunction and premature ejaculation. Finally, only after clinicians and researchers began to examine gay relationship dynamics was a natural bridge formed that led to the topic of sexual functioning within couples. We are now more than ever aware of the quieter and sometimes purposefully hidden sexual problems that can occur for a male or between the men in a couple.

The most prevalent sexual conditions for men (regardless of orientation) are erectile dysfunction, premature ejaculation, orgasmic disorder (delayed ejaculation to the point of frustration and/or pain or the inability to ejaculate), Peyronie's Disease (extreme curvature of the penis caused by a buildup of plaque within it), priapism (an erection lasting more than four hours, which can lead to cell death of muscles in the penis), and, finally, the category "sexual desire disorders" under which are listed two other dysfunctions. First, hypoactive sexual desire disorder, described as a persistent lack of sexual fantasies and desire for sexual activity. Second, sexual aversion disorder described as aversion and avoidance of contact with the genitals of a sexual partner.

Each of the above conditions can influence sexual satisfaction for a couple. A couple can be dissatisfied with their sex life based on problems such as premature ejaculation and erectile dysfunction that have been evident from the earliest stages of the relationship. Conversely, after years of sexual satisfaction a couple may now need guidance; for example, this could occur after surgical treatment of the prostrate that leads to erectile dysfunction. With regard to sexual desire, couples most often experience dissatisfaction based on the presence of sexual discrepancy: one partner demonstrates more interest and desire for sex than the other. While this can occur early on in a relationship, a more typical scenario occurs when one or both partners exhibit a markedly decreased interest in sexual activity after a period of mutual sexual satisfaction. This could arise from recent medical complications (e.g., antidepressant and cancer treatments) or be indicative of diminished sexual passion (at least for our present partner) associated with long-term relationships.

Assessment

The first step in treating sexual dissatisfaction in a couple is a comprehensive assessment. In the case of reduced sexual desire, sexologists attempt to ascertain patterns in a presenting couple. Is it lifelong or acquired? Is it generalized in that there is a broad lack of interest in sexual activity, or is it situational in that desire is lacking only in specific situations? For many gay men, a lack of sexual desire is specific to their current partner and they are otherwise capable of experiencing desire, whether in fantasy or real life, for a new sex partner with no problem. If, however, one or both men are experiencing a general loss of sexual desire in all areas of life as evidenced by decreased sexual involvement with each other, masturbation, and sexual fantasies, both elaborate and fleeting, a medical examination is suggested. Is antidepressant treatment the cause? Low testosterone? An underlying medical problem that has gone undiagnosed? Is substance abuse occurring? Has a recent injury occurred? A decrease in overall sexual desire could well be indicative of a medical issue. Also, if a male begins to experience diagnosable dysfunctions such as premature ejaculation or delayed ejaculation after a long period of non-problematic sexual functioning, these too could indicate an underlying medical etiology. A partner, though, who only exhibits a lack of sexual desire or sexual dysfunction in his current relationship but who is more than capable and ready to engage in carnal involvements with other men can move on to the next question.

The second is a matter that we might for take for granted, but which we shouldn't: Do both men in the couple want to improve their sexual relationship with each other? Typically it is long-term couples who enter treatment for sexual difficulties. Couples still in the early stages of a relationship who do experience sexual dissatisfaction often end the relationship. Working on sexual problems requires commitment and investment in a relationship. Some male couples enter treatment mutually anxious to resolve mounting sexual dissatisfaction. Others seek treatment at the urging of one male in the relationship or due to his unequivocal ultimatum that their sex life improves or the relationship ends. But if one partner is involved in a clandestine affair, is in love with another person, is already planning to leave but is waiting for the right moment to spring this information, or, for any other number of reasons, is not invested in improving sexual satisfaction within his current relationship, the outcome is predetermined to be unsuccessful. For readers looking to enrich their sex lives, it's time for an open dialogue on just this topic. Improved sexual satisfaction will not occur without a commitment from both men; both must be open to improving sexual satisfaction. It is both common and acceptable for one man to desire this outcome more than the other, but as long as both are willing to sincerely try for increased sexual satisfaction, positive change is possible. And what if one partner stubbornly refuses to engage in this exploration? If it reaches this point, both men must candidly discuss their expectations for the future of the relationship.

Since the fields of medicine and psychology are fond of classification systems, it probably won't be too surprising to learn that there are categories that sort different etiological factors affecting sexual dissatisfaction. First we have those predominantly medical factors that result in sexual dysfunctions. Second we have individual issues that affect a couple's sexual satisfaction. And finally we have those relationship issues that too can lead to dissatisfaction in the bedroom. Readers are cautioned to remember that these often overlap and that there is no definitive and impenetrable boundary between the categories. For example, delayed ejaculation may be caused by medical issues, but it can lead to reluctance to engage in sex, thus resulting in ever more sexual dissatisfaction within a couple.

Medical Dysfunctions

When a couple begins to examine dissatisfaction, questions to consider include:

- *Is sexual satisfaction affected by erectile dysfunction, premature ejaculation, an inability to ejaculate or reach orgasm, and/or pain during sex?*
- *Has there been a marked decrease in sexual desire not circumscribed only to one's current partner? In other words, does a man have less interest and less involvement in masturbation, sexual fantasy, and use of pornography in addition to a lack of sexual desire in the relationship?*

- *Are there known etiological explanations for these conditions, including:*

  Alcohol or other substance use?

  A recent injury that could affect sexual functioning? For example, current research finds that head traumas can affect hormone levels, including sex hormones.

  Medical problems such as diabetes or cardiovascular concerns?

  Mental health issues, particularly depression?

  Treatment for a medical condition that affects sexual functioning? Recall that many of the most popular medications for depression have a deleterious effect on sexual desire and produce an inability to ejaculate and that prostate surgery can result in erectile problems.

  Age-related changes, including a drop in testosterone levels? The prevalence of erectile dysfunction and lack of sexual desire increases with age, most notably after fifty.

Intrapersonal Factors

Now let's examine what professionals call intrapsychic issues, those psychological issues emanating from within an individual.

- *Is there evidence of internalized homophobia? This can lead to an inability to feel positive about both oneself and other gay men. Relationships are often unsatisfying, and intimacy is impossible. Sex with strangers is frequently sought rather than with an intimate partner.*

- *Is a man too invested in a stereotypical male role? Believing that one must exhibit limited emotion, including tenderness and affection, and remain strong and independent at all times and in all circumstances has been found to lead to sexual dissatisfaction. Such a stance can lead to disagreement in a couple regarding sexual practices (Who will be the dominant partner?) and reduce intimacy, a recognized factor in sexual satisfaction.*

- *Are there unresolved issues surrounding childhood abuse and trauma, especially sexual abuse? Childhood abuse can lead to an inability to trust, decreased sexual desire, an inability to form intimate connections with another person, the need to pull away if intimacy begins, and the ability to only engage in sexual activity with a person for whom they have no intimate feelings.*

- *Are there unaddressed sexual fetish or sexual orientation issues? One of the possible factors affecting decreased sexual desire in a heterosexual couple is the presence of a hidden sexual fetish. Does cross-dressing turn on a male? Is his preference for children? Also, is a married "straight" man really sexually attracted to other males? We must at least consider the same possibility for gay men. Though it is unlikely that gay men have a hidden preference for women that is affecting their sex lives with a current male partner, there could be a primary attraction to children, animals, or a host of fetishes, such as cross-dressing, sexual activity involving urine and feces, or a host of other "kinks." If a partner is unable to obtain sexual gratification from his primary sexual preferences—either because it could result in legal difficulties, his partner is unwilling to explore these activities, or the male himself is to embarrassed to ask for this type of gratifi-*

cation in the relationship - his contentment with an unwilling or unknowing partner will eventually diminish.

- Are there unresolved childhood issues? Parents who are intrusive, disrespectful of boundaries, manipulative, and possessive can interfere with a child's ability to develop a stable identity. The literature is replete with case examples of men who had to assume the role of a placeholder husband for their mothers in their parents' dysfunctional relationships. These youths grow into men confused about or incapable of intimacy; becoming too close—even sexually—can be overwhelming. At a less profound level, parents also overtly and covertly teach messages about sex that their children cannot help but internalize. Children might learn that sex is "dirty" or that it is something that has to be done but is certainly not to be enjoyed.

- Are there unresolved past relationship issues? Have one or both men recently lost a partner through a breakup or death? It is certainly possible that the emotions associated with this loss are still present and interfere with sexual satisfaction in the current relationship. It would be difficult for a man to make love to his current partner if, all the while, he is distracted by thoughts of a past love.

- Is stress external to the relationship affecting one or both partners? Stress resulting from myriad and possibly concurrent events (e.g., relocating, the illness or death of a parent, financial concerns) can cause a marked decrease in sexual desire and motivation.

- Is fatigue affecting sexual desire? One or both men in the couple might simply be exhausted from their daily routines or from a current stressful life occurrence. Sexual involvement is the last thing they crave.

- *Does one of the men (or even both) spend too much time looking at pornography, particularly online? Couples are learning that a computer can become a sexual rival. Since pornography is so often associated with masturbation, solo (and often secret) orgasm may well interfere with partnered sex. This is especially true for men over the age of forty due to the need for an extended refractory period.*

- *Are there underlying fears about disease and contamination? With rates of HIV and almost all sexually transmitted diseases on the rise in the gay community, even those in established relationships may be fearful of infection. This is even truer for couples engaged in open relationships or for those men who doubt that their partners are truly monogamous. A man may be fretful that he will either contract HIV or other disease or, conversely, give one to his partner.*

- *Are there body image concerns? Are one or both men embarrassed or uncomfortable with their bodies in general or specific aspects of the body? Penis size and weight top the list of these concerns in regard to sexual activity. A male's discomfort, and regrettably, sometimes even shame over his self-determined deficiencies can interfere with his ability to experience and offer sexual pleasure.*

- *Are there sexual performance concerns? The topic of spectatoring, monitoring oneself during sexual activity instead of fully participating in the act, is common and was introduced earlier in this book. A man might be so worried about technique or timing of ejaculation that his ability to actually enjoy sex is diminished. His thoughts interfere with satisfaction.*

- *Are there unrealistic expectations about sexual activity? Too many men have expectations about sexual activity based on scenes and images from adult sexual videos and magazines. In these depictions, a sex act ends with a shattering orgasm leaving both men (and possibly more) shuddering in a pool of sweat and semen-coated sheets. This does happen, but for most men, not consistently. Sexual activity can be fulfilling and pleasurable even without the drama and noise inherent in adult male videos. But a man who has an expectation that this is what sex should be like is bound to be disappointed.*

Relationship Issues

Sexologists have learned that sexual dissatisfaction is often an overt manifestation of numerous underlying relationship issues. A couple might be dismayed by sexual dissatisfaction, but this concern is the veritable tip of the iceberg. Sexual satisfaction is not likely to move in a positive direction until these issues are explored and resolved. The passion that inflames the relationship early on hides these issues, at least temporarily.

- *Is there a difference in identity development between the two men? Gay men follow a trajectory of identity formation that optimally leads to acceptance and pride. However, some men become stuck at one stage along this developmental path, and some take a much longer time than others moving from stage to stage. Thus if we have a male couple consisting of two men who self-describe as "gay" we still cannot assume that they are the same level of development. For example, Duncan is a gay man who is out and proud. But his partner, Wayne, is definitely not proud that he is gay.*

158

Though he has come to recognize that he cannot change his erotic orientation after two past attempts at reparative therapies (including hypnosis), he is still ashamed of being gay. Indeed, if an intervention was developed that could unfailingly change his orientation, he would be the first in line for treatment.

- *Is there a discrepancy between the sex drive / libido of the two men in the couple? Clinical literature relates that sexual desire discrepancies are very common in male couples, and it is rare for partners to have an equal amount of sexual interest in each other. In spite of this being a rather commonplace occurrence, it is still frequently a cause of sexual and relationship dissatisfaction for both men. The high-interest partner is frustrated because the other is unwilling to engage in sex or, if he does oblige, exhibits little interest. Our low-drive man feels resentment that he is being sexually manipulated in spite of his own wishes. "Let's just get it over with," is his thought. Note that a low-interest partner may have little desire for sex because this is his biological make-up or due to one or more of the reasons listed in the medical dysfunctions, intrapersonal, and/or other relationship concerns. The high-interest partner is not off the hook either. He too may be biologically primed to have a copious libido, but we must ferret out whether there is evidence of sexual compulsivity or the use of sex as a means of self-soothing of negative emotions brought on by his own intrapersonal issues.*

- *Are one or both partners inexperienced, unaccomplished, or ineffective in the act of lovemaking? LoPiccolo and Friedman (1988) presented a wonderful vignette of a heterosexual couple that is still very informative for our purposes. A wife complained that her husband was extremely clumsy during sexual activity, and she often ended up with bruises. No, this was not purposeful S&M. She "complained that her husband stuck his fingers into her eye; inadvertently pulled her hair; stuck his elbow into her neck, chest, or ribs; gave her bruises in the legs by accidentally banging his knees into her." The therapist was judiciously cautious in allocating all responsibility on the male; after all, he did not know this couple well enough to determine the veracity of the wife's report. However, during the first session with the husband present, the husband dropped a cup of coffee onto a glass table top, thus shattering it, and tripped into a large potted plant. At this juncture the therapist began to believe the wife's report.*

- *This book has already discussed the issue of sexual skills and, often, their lack. A male might indeed be awkward and clumsy during sexual activity. Again, there is a widespread belief that gay men are instinctively skilled at sex. This is definitely not the case, and there are as many fumbling and unskilled gay males as there are straight males.*

- *Is there some type of sexual aversion or distaste for specific acts that is affecting the sexual dynamics of the relationship? This chapter has already mentioned sexual aversion disorder which closely resembles a phobia of genital contact. Less severe, but still problematic, is an aversion to specific acts. According to Margaret Nichols and Michael Shernoff in their review of sex therapy with sexual minorities, the most prevalent is a repugnance with oral and/or anal sex.*

- *Are there differing motivations for sex? One partner may define sexual activity as a form of intimacy; he is not focused on orgasm as much as closeness and sharing. Reaching orgasm is certainly a great additional frill but is not as*

*meaningful as a shared mutual moment between two part-
ners. Other men may use sex as a mean of assuaging anxiety
and other unpleasant emotions. Still others use sex as a
means to demonstrate prowess, to prove their attractiveness,
or due to a compulsive need for sexual engagement. And
reasons can change. The man who typically appreciates sex
as a means of sharing may be feeling particularly aroused
after attending a party that featured a male stripper, and
the male who is almost always focused on orgasm may turn
to his lover for the intimacy exhibited in sex when faced
with an illness in his immediate family. However, a fairly
unchanging discrepancy between two men as to their motivations for sex can result in dissatisfaction. The man who
desires intimacy will eventually be turned off by a partner
who uses sex as a means of self-gratification. Likewise, the
latter will become irritated with his partner's need for sharing, cuddling, and constant desire to fashion sex into a display of love.*

- *Is there conflict in the relationship? Leiblum and Rosen
(1988) equate the loss of sexual desire in one or both partners to a fever: a high fever indicates that something is
wrong but in itself is not a diagnosis. A loss of sexual desire
and the dissatisfaction that comes with it are often only
symptoms of much more pertinent relationship issues. These
issues can be those common to all couples (e.g., time constraints, problems with in-laws, money issues, poor communication skills, power differences) or those specific to male
couples as were presented in Chapter Two.*
- *Are one or both men in the couple bored with the current
sexual repertoire? The field of sexual enrichment stipulates
that a sexual relationship between two partners must grow*

and change or otherwise risk boring partners into a state of sexual apathy (at least within the relationship; these same men would have no problem experiencing desire for other men).

- *Is one partner overweight or out of shape? We're not talking a few pounds here. Research finds that a physical lack of attraction to a partner due to weigh gain can lead to diminished desire. Sex researchers Bob Berkowitz and Susan Yager-Berkowitz (2008) summed up this predicament: It seems "illogical that one can gain a great deal of weight and adopt a less than healthy lifestyle and still expect to be desired with frequency and great passion" (p. 170).*
- *Is there sexual activity and/or another romantic relationship occurring outside of the primary relationship, either covertly or acknowledged by both partners, that is detracting from sexual satisfaction?*

We often spend so much time examining the negative factors that impinge on our sexual satisfaction that we forget to examine the idiosyncratic definitions of "good sex" held by each man in a couple. Just what does satisfying sex mean for each individual person? In his book *The New Male Sexuality* (1999), Zilderberg states that there are some common conditions for satisfying sex, and, in addition, each man has his own personal constellation of conditions for what he considers good sex. An assessment should include an examination of these factors, including specific environmental conditions, specific sexual acts, and foreplay and post-sexual activity behaviors.

Once we become aware of sexual dissatisfaction in our relationship—whether this is a sudden occurrence, has been present since the early days of the relationship, or has been building over time—we need to understand why. What is causing the dissatisfaction? Possibly there is one and only one underlying factor, but more likely there are several variables occurring simultaneously. The last several pages have offered a veritable catalogue of issues known to affect sexual dissatisfaction. Scrutinize each one. Which ones seem valid, and which have no bearing at all? Many of these proposed etiological factors can be immediately disregarded, and most couples can narrow the list down to a few that may be relevant.

For those couples that seek the assistance of a therapist to guide a sexual satisfaction intervention, this professional will spend a number of sessions evaluating your relationship for these very same concerns as well as monitoring your interactions while in the confines of the office; these may offer evidence of possible relationship problems. For example, one male seems to dominate the conversation and interrupts his partner even when he does offer input; such a communication pattern is quite instructive for the therapist regarding the day-to-day dynamics of the couple and can hold valuable information as to why sexual dissatisfaction is occurring.

Treatment

Based on the outcomes of our assessment of sexual dissatisfaction, interventions often become obvious. Relationship issues require a couples intervention, a health problem necessitates medical intercession, and residual emotional issues and childhood baggage still lingering in our psyche and interfering in our lives may demand individual therapy. Self-help books can assist with many of these issues. I also suggest that readers who are experiencing sexual dissatisfaction consider sexual enrichment interventions. The next section will offer an overview of sexual enrichment, or in other words, methods and interventions to increase sexual satisfaction in our ongoing relationship.

Sexual Satisfaction Defined

Many couples will need to work on sexual enhancement and enrichment; sexual dissatisfaction has become such a chronic condition that sexual activity is completely avoided, at least with a partner. Couples need to avoid forestalling intimate contact with each other and proactively seek to find its pleasurable aspects once again. Even for those men in open relationships, maintaining pleasurable sexual involvement with a primary partner denotes the continual relevance and importance of a relationship and can help minimize nagging suspicions that a new and better lover has taken one's place.

To start, an understanding of sexual dissatisfaction must be prefaced by the possibility of satisfying and healthy sexual relating, and there is no paucity of definitions for a "healthy sexual relationship." The Sexuality Information and Education Council of the United States (SIECUS) formulated guidelines for comprehensive sexuality education that have become one of the most trusted resources for educators. One of its key concepts is that "sexuality is a central part of being human, and individuals express their sexuality in a variety of ways." Sadly, many adults do not have a basic understanding of this key concept, the very same that SIECUS attempts to instill in children.

As a foundation for satisfying sexual relationships throughout our lives, SIECUS proposes the following:

- *We should take responsibility for our own sexual behavior.*
- *We should enjoy and express sexuality throughout life.*
- *We should express our sexuality in ways that are congruent with our values.*
- *We should discriminate between life-enhancing sexual behaviors and those that are harmful to self and/or others.*
- *We should be able to express our sexuality while respecting the rights of others.*
- *We should seek new information to enhance our sexuality.*
- *We should engage in sexual relationships that are consensual, non-exploitative, honest, pleasurable, and protected.*

Note that this is only one entity's definition of healthy sexuality, but almost all of the core requirements shared by differing definitions are present in that of SEICUS, particularly a focus on pleasure, consent, non-exploitation, mutuality, and the need to be cognizant and proactive in seeking new information that can increase sexual satisfaction and growth. Other definitions of healthy sexual relations clarify some of the inherent though not clearly enunciated principles of SIECUS. For example, definitions often list individuality, a recognition that each person has his or her own sexual desires, concerns, goals, and boundaries. Pressuring a partner to subscribe to our own wants and desires regardless of what he wants is not conducive to long-term sexual satisfaction and compatibility. Not forgetting that our partner is a separate being and not merely an accessory in our own lives is essential, but as relationships progress through the years, we do often begin to take our partners for granted. We forget their depth and we become unwelcoming to surprises in their characters.

Men in a relationship need to clarify what they do and do not want and what they like and don't like with regard to sexual activity. Open dialogue, while highly recommended and indeed the only meaningful method for learning about the satisfactions and dissatisfactions in our relationship, is not as easy as it ostensibly seems. In fact, we know that for many couples, such a dialogue is improbable due to one or both partner's defensiveness. More than one professional working with couples on sexual concerns has stated that openness and nondefensiveness are the two qualities most essential for achieving sexual satisfaction. Each male in the couple must be receptive to feedback without being guarded, critical, retaliatory, and hypersensitive. Each must be open to hearing what his partner vouchsafes. Many couples have experienced a decrease in their sexual satisfaction obvious to both partners, yet this is never broached, at least within the parameters of the relationship. A male may share his sexual dissatisfaction with friends or even a hidden lover on the side, but the possibility of sharing sexual concerns with his partner is never considered. Discussions of sex are already fraught with discomfort simply because culture has made sex an uncomfortable topic; when we then have to factor in predictions about a partner's responses such as anger, defensiveness, or hurt, it is simply easier to suffer silently all the while with a growing amount of resentment and concomitant attenuating sexual satisfaction.

Dialogues about sex do not have to be only about dissatisfaction, and they can instead focus on fantasies, changing desires, and dreams. It is quite possible that the male that has always shunned anal sex has decided to explore the possibility;

he is certainly not ready for penetration and may decide after consideration that this really isn't what he wants. But what a loss for two men who have voluntarily comingled their lives if they are unable to share their shifting desires and temporary fantasies even if they are never acted upon. Healthy sexual relationships acknowledge that partners change, including sexual desires and motivations.

The following list is a summary of the most pressing qualities and characteristics associated with long-term sexual satisfaction within a relationship:

- *Personal responsibility*
- *Openness*
- *Nondefensiveness*
- *Honesty*
- *Compassion*
- *Respect for a partner as a separate individual*
- *Empathy*
- *Vulnerability*
- *Seeking out information that enhances sexual satisfaction*
- *A recognition that our desire and sexual motivations fluctuate and change*
- *Willingness to try new things*
- *Willingness to change*
- *Sexual relationships are consensual, non-exploitative, and pleasurable*

Sexual Enrichment Interventions

In the field of sex therapy, most practitioners aim to resolve a presenting sexual problem with a brief intervention. If this brief intervention is not successful, they then move on to a considerably more involved and intensive treatment protocol. This section takes the same approach. If the interventions in this section do not increase sexual satisfaction, we may be looking at much deeper issues that will necessitate intensive therapy. Issues such as childhood sexual abuse, the effects of trauma, alcohol and/or substance dependence, compulsive sexual behaviors, hidden infidelity, profound internalized homophobia, longstanding relationship conflict, and, of course, medical problems often require attention before increased sexual satisfaction is possible.

Information

Remarkably, many sexual problems can be ameliorated and even completely resolved with the simple use of education. Sex education in this country is abysmal, and many gay men learn about sex through trial and error. When we add in the fact that many gay men begin sexual and relationship exploration far later than their straight peers, it's not coincidental that we often don't have an accurate idea of sexual functioning and expression. I've worked with enough gay men to realize that their image—even their ideal of hot sex—is based on scenarios seen in adult videos. Education is thus imperative.

When sexual dissatisfaction occurs, unwanted beliefs about the relationship may arise, most often that this is a sign that the relationship is coming to an end or that great sex can never happen again with a partner. Thus a good starting point is to establish a foundation of more optimistic and reasonable beliefs including:

- *Sexual satisfaction is only one component of a successful relationship.*
- *Most partnered couples do not have an equal sexual desire for each other; a committed long-lasting relationship does not require equal levels of interest in sex.*
- *Our levels of sexual desire and interest change, sometimes abruptly or over an extended period of time.*
- *There are interventions to augment sexual satisfaction.*

Information can take on many forms. First, information is often focused on problems detected in the assessment. For example, a couple might learn about the effects of drug and alcohol use, stress and fatigue, and antidepressant medications on sexual desire and satisfaction. The recurrent issues of internalized homophobia and rigid stereotypical sex roles, so often a presence in male couples, can also be addressed via education if these are noted as problems in the assessment. Second, a couple can also benefit from learning about male sexual functioning and expression in general, including the inevitability of sexual boredom with a current partner, the change from passion to companionate love, and common sexual myths including:

- *Orgasm is the ultimate and often only goal of sexual activity. Instead, sexually satisfied couples focus on the process rather than the outcome.*
- *A good sexual relationship is determined by the amount of sex that occurs. The reality is that quality often trumps quantity.*
- *Good sex is spontaneous. As stated by Perel (2006), "I urge my patients not to be spontaneous about sex. Spontaneity is a fabulous idea, but in an ongoing relationship whatever is*

going to "just happen" already has. Now they have to make it happen. Committed sex is intentional sex." Premeditated sex is not of lesser quality than that of spontaneous sex.

- *The need for manual stimulation to obtain an erection is a capitulation of bodily prowess and sexual power. As young men we are accustomed to instant erections that do not require manual stimulation by either ourselves or our partners, but older men very often cannot rely on spontaneous erections. This is a natural sexual transition for males and not a sign of weakness or an indication of relationship problems.*

Men may also need to learn about general factors that affect the sexual satisfaction of all couples, including scheduling sexual activity and proactively creating an environment conducive for this activity. For many couples the issue of timing begins to affect their sexual interactions. For example, Evan has to be at work at 7:00 a.m., and to make his morning routine less complicated, he showers and shaves each night before he goes to bed. His partner James finds that he is most sexually aroused in the morning but is unable to cajole Evan into even a quickie at this time. Evan refuses; this is simply not a good time for sex for him. Of course, a simple dialogue about timing would assist this couple, but they, like so many others, refuse to engage in such an exchange. To even consider having to schedule sex imperils their belief in the supremacy of spontaneity.

In addition to scheduling, couples can create an environment that is mutually conducive to sexual activity. Walt had two male roommates, and he became even more sexually aroused knowing that they could hear him while engaged in his vigorous sex sessions. However, once he met Shawn, a contrast became evident. Shawn was uncomfortable with the knowledge that other men might be listening to their sexual encounters. Indeed, he spent much of their time together trying to hush Walt up. Shawn had not the slightest exhibitionistic streak. Thus an intervention for these men would be to create an erotic environment that is agreeable to all involved. Even something as banal as keeping lights on during sex can pose a challenge to sexual satisfaction for many men.

The combination of education and open dialogue between the involved men can be effective—sometimes completely and other times only partially—with many of the concerns that were discussed in the assessment section of this chapter, including stress and fatigue, ineffective sexual techniques, sexual performance anxiety and spectatoring, distaste for specific sexual acts, unrealistic expectations about sexual performance, and fears of contamination. If education and dialogue alone are not sufficient, a couple can move onto more intensive interventions.

Homework Assignments

For some sexual problems and challenges, information by itself will not bring about a resolution. Consider the aversion to anal sexual involvement so often encountered in male couples. Learning that this is common may offer some succor but does not, by itself, resolve the problem. One option is for a couple to find alternative sexual methods, satisfying to both men, that avoid anal involvement. Other couples may choose an alternative solution in which the male who has the aversion gradually explores anal involvement in sexual activity. This can start off with him touching his own anus, moving on to allowing his partner to perform this touch, to allowing insertion of a finger, to, finally, a penis. The man has complete power to stop at any time and may ultimately decide that anal involvement isn't enjoyable after all. On the other hand, he may learn to enjoy and even relish it.

As another example, couples coping with premature ejaculation can practice the squeeze technique in which the penis is squeezed with the thumb and the forefinger just below the corona of the head of the penis. Use of this technique can allow for fifteen to twenty minutes of sexual activity before ejaculation occurs. Finally, couples that discern problematic relationship issues as the cause of their sexual dissatisfaction can practice new communication skills and a host of other new nonsexual behaviors.

For every issue described in this chapter, there is available information and pragmatic suggestions for overcoming them. The Resources section at the end of this book will offer some suggestions to begin your search. In sum, information and behavioral practice can often overcome even some of the most refractory issues.

Change Existing Sexual Routines

A recurrent suggestion to revive passion is to add variety and make purposeful change in existing sexual habits. In other words, shake up the routine a bit. For example, David Schnarch, in the book *Resurrecting Sex* (2002), explains that every once in a while the sexual relationship has to be shaken up and that these periodic perturbations must be incorporated into the pattern of a long-term relationship. Sex researchers Bob Berkowitz and Susan Yager-Berkowitz prescribe broadening our definition of sex so as to include myriad erotic activities.

I discussed the process of changing sexual routines with Michael Shernoff, a renowned male couples therapist and author of eight books on various aspects of gay male sexuality. Shernoff is in the seventh year of a monogamous relationship, and though he and his partner have jokingly contemplated the addition of a third person for sex, both have agreed that this is not necessary. When I asked him how he and his partner have managed to maintain the sexual spark that their relationship reflects, he informed me that during the sexual heyday of the 1970s, one of the most flattering compliments that could be applied to a gay man was the appellation "pig." And this had nothing to do with weight or being a police officer. "A 'pig,'" Shernoff said, "was somebody who felt no need for sexual manners. They could get nasty, and involve themselves in endless sexual adventures (and misadventures). They weren't ashamed of sex at all." Shernoff coaches men in a couple to get in there and get dirty once again with each other as a means of maintaining sexual satisfaction.

But sexual shake-ups are more difficult than they sound. In Shernoff's perspective, our culture is nearly phobic about sex. We have to work on overcoming our own sexual concerns and doubts and focus instead on rejoicing in the unadulterated nastiness of sex if we are to maintain a high level of sexual satisfaction. The reality, though, is that we tend to become even more uncomfortable in altering sexual routines with our partners as the relationship endures. During the delirium of passion, we are able to override internal conflicts and restraints about sex; we are able to ignore all the derogatory messages about sex that we learned through childhood and equally disregard our own concerns about our bodies, our performance, and ourselves in general. Yet once passion attenuates, the diminishment of the neurochemical rush allows all of these lurking fears and concerns to resurface.

While I had Shernoff on the phone, I took the opportunity to ask his views on long-term monogamy. He too finds that there is an increasing number of couples seeking monogamy but failing at it. He concluded that a lack of norms and models for gay monogamy are a decisive cause for this repeated scenario. He too admitted that even for him and his partner, sexual passion is not the same as it was during the early stages of their relationship. Sex is still wonderful, incredible, and satisfying, but it is different. He teaches couples that a decrease in the awe-inspiring passion of the honeymoon period is not an omen that the relationship is over. Instead, it's a sign of the need to work on creativity, experimentation, and increasing vulnerability. Michael LaSala, Fulbright Scholar and Associate Professor in the School of Social Work at Rutgers University, echoed this prescription: couples succeed by "introducing new ideas into their sex (videos, role plays, toys, BD/SM if relevant). The couples whose sex life has fizzled are those who failed to do this."

In her witty book *Mating in Captivity* (2006), Esther Perel too offers similar advice. She reports that she finds that even in couples where sex has stopped completely, both partners still maintain active sexual desire as evidenced by masturbation, daydreams, fantasies, and arousal to a person they pass on the street or wait in line behind at the pharmacy. The individuals in a couple become erotically numb to each other but not to others. One of her suggestions to couples is to bring creativity and erotic imagination back into sexual activity; we have to enter and honor the erotic minds and fantasies of each other. And this could mean getting "nasty" and allowing oneself to be a "pig."

Perel wisely counsels, though, that sometimes knowing the fantasies of our partner can put sexual satisfaction even more out of reach. Learning that our lover is actually fantasizing about having sex with various four-legged friends while his penis in thrusting back and forth within us may lead to abhorrence and horror. Sometimes a stunning discovery can be an aphrodisiac while at other times it can lead to apoplexy.

Sensate Focus

This procedure is the cornerstone of all sex therapy interventions, and most couples experiencing sexual dissatisfaction can benefit from it. It is strongly recommended for couples in which sexual involvement between the two partners has completely or almost completely stopped. Its goal is to gradually enable a couple to focus on the myriad pleasurable sensations associated with sexual activity rather than the outcome of orgasm. Sensate focus takes place in a comfortable and safe environment conducive to intimacy for both partners, and both men agree to temporarily forego their established sexual repertoire in order to relearn and practice the basics of intimacy, affection, and the offering and receiving of pleasure. Due to the purposefully planned gradual nature of sensate focus, the process unfolds over several weeks. During the period of sensate focus, other ongoing attempts at sexual involvement within the couple should stop.

Step One: Nongenital Pleasuring: Touching each other with clothes on. The goal here it to reintroduce physical contact between two men that is not threatening or noxious to either. Behaviors include holding hands and back rubs (with clothes on). Couples that already engage in these behaviors without a problem can quickly move on to the next step but otherwise it is suggested that a couple practice for three weeks with two sessions per week. Each session should last approximate sixty minutes, with each partner receiving and giving touch for thirty minutes. If during this first stage of nongenital touching, a partner becomes aroused and desirous of furthering the activity to genital touching, the response is a firm "no." Remember, the purpose of sensate focus it to help a couple move away from orgasm as the goal of sexual activity. Also, for Steps One and Two, minimize conversation and dialogue. Discussions of the experience can occur afterward.

Step Two: Genital Pleasuring: Men in a couple are encouraged to touch each other in areas noted for sexual response. There are no off-limits areas unless one partner does not enjoy stimulation of specific areas. This can include oral contact if one or both men find it pleasurable. The goal, however, is NOT erection or orgasm but rather re-experiencing the ability to offer and receive pleasure. Helping each other to enjoy bodily sensations is paramount. This is a wonderful opportunity for men to communicate with each other about what does and does not turn them on. Again, take several weeks with this process.

Step Three: Orgasm: Finally, men may engage in activities learned in the first two stages of sensate focus that may bring about orgasm; recall, though, that is not the ultimate *goal but rather an enjoyment of physical sensations. This is also an opportunity to experiment with new sexual experiences.*

The use of sensate focus helps a couple vary longstanding sexual repertoires, clearly state what they do and do not like, guide a partner physically as to what offers pleasure, experience this pleasure, and respect each other's boundaries. All of these are essential for healthy sexual relationships.

Cognitive Restructuring

This refers to reducing interfering and distracting thoughts that affect sexual satisfaction. Worrying about one's body, the firmness of an erection, or tomorrow's deadline at work while engaged in the act of sexual activity is not conducive to sexual satisfaction. A sexual fantasy about a past lover while engaged in the act with a current partner may increase our arousal or may deflate it entirely. Recalling last night's unresolved argument can make us lose all desire for sexual intimacy. Intrusive thoughts can occur prior, during, and even after sexual involvement. The goal of this sexual enrichment intervention, then, is to identify these thoughts and reduce or, better yet, eliminate them.

Research tells us that a person may have a pattern or several patterns of thoughts that interfere with sexual satisfaction. Cognitive restructuring is focused on repetitive interfering thought patterns. Common patterns include:

- *Negative thoughts about one's body.*
- *Negative thoughts about one's sexual performance.*

- *Negative thoughts about one's partner.*
- *Negative thoughts about sexual activity in general ("Sexual activity is disgusting.").*
- *Self-protective thoughts such as a partner can't be trusted or will hurt me in the future.*
- *Distractions from other concerns in life.*

Men are coached to create a list of these thoughts, to verbalize them aloud, and to create more accurate and beneficial responses to them. However, often these repetitive thought patterns are a manifestation of underlying problems such as internalized homophobia; disputing these thoughts does not necessarily resolve their root cause, and individual therapy or therapeutic self-help may be needed. But let us not be purposefully blind to the fact that thoughts may be a reflection of reality. Maybe a partner isn't good at sexual activity, maybe one's weight does make one feel unattractive and unhealthy, and maybe a partner can't be trusted based on his past behaviors.

State-of-the Art Interventions for Sexual Enrichment

Sensate focus and cognitive restructuring have been staples of sexual enrichment for decades, and education and relationship counseling have been in existence far longer. Though they have not remained static and monolithic approaches and have indeed developed when research indicated a need for modification, still many of their core principles remain unaltered. This next section will offer a summary of what the most current research offers with regard to sexual enrichment. You will note that all focus on altering neurochemicals in the brain.

- *Evaluate use of antidepressants—The most popular antide-pressant medications on the market are SSRIs (Selective Serotonin Reuptake Inhibitors). Chances are that if you're on an anti-depressant, you are taking an SSRI. While these drugs are much safer than past pharmaceuticals for depres-sion, they do have noted common side effects, most particu-larly on sexual expression. An estimated 70 percent of SSRI users report diminished libido, inability to achieve an erec-tion, and/or delayed, diminished, or eliminated ability to ejaculate. In other words, men using these medications lose their sexual desire or experience frustration with perfor-mance during sex, affecting both themselves and their part-ners. I even work with men who have become frustrated in their attempts at masturbation in that they simply cannot ejaculate.*
- *Do not stop taking your antidepressant medications until you and your doctor discuss options—For some people, sex-ual side effects are worth enduring in comparison to the symptoms of depression. There are, however, other medica-tions that can be substituted or even added to the current regimen to increase dopamine levels in the brain, the same neurochemical found to be prevalent during passion. If your sex life has been severely hampered by antidepressant usage, it might be worth reassessing options with a profes-sional.*
- *Engage in novel and anxiety-provoking situations—So many couples report that sexual satisfaction increases, albeit temporarily, while on a vacation. While some of this is due to a removal of the surroundings that have become over-associated with sexual apathy and ennui, we now also know that novelty and/or danger elevate dopamine levels in the*

brain. *Relationship therapists now regularly advise couples to try new activities, particularly those that promote anxiety. John, for example, surprisingly found himself engaged in an episode of great sex with his partner after he finished a public speaking assignment, an act that terrified him. Roller coasters, scary films, and bungee jumping are known to affect dopamine levels, the neurochemical that stimulates passion and arousal. And for those who would never even contemplate bungee jumping or a two-loop roller coaster, less dramatic options are still available. The more couples change their routine and schedule, the more they engage in last-minute or novel activities, the more likely passion will reemerge. Variety is not only the spice of life; it is also a stimulant for desire.*

- *Engage in sex with a partner even if desire is absent—It is only recently that researchers noted a common sexual arousal pattern in females: a woman often experiences sexual arousal prior to experiencing desire. Men often are the reverse; desire preceded arousal. We may see an attractive male or a fantasy may traipse unannounced into our mind, and before we know it, we have an erection. The corollary to this is that even if we do not have sexual desire for a partner, if we nevertheless begin sexual activity, desire may well follow. The men I work with who have a fetish of seducing straight men absolutely support this contention. They report that they start off by trying to sexually arouse their prey, and once excited enough, the desire for some type of sexual involvement—often oral sex—is destined to occur.*

- *We also know that orgasms stimulate production of vasopressin, a neurohormone that primarily affects kidney func-*

tioning, but which is also known to stimulate attachment, love, and warm feelings for our partner. From this we can surmise that couples who have more orgasms also maintain higher levels of desire for each other.

- *Have more physical contact with each other*—Stroking, touching, massage, and even prolonged eye contact of more than two minutes have all been found to stimulate chemical changes in the brain that promote desire.
- *Enhance your physical and mental health*—Maintaining a fit body and mind are conducive to sexual satisfaction. And at a more basic prurient level, we already know that physical attractiveness is a primary sexual turn-on for males. An out-of-shape body is certainly not a visual stimulant for male desire.
- *Delay sexual activity*—Placing a ban on sexual activity may paradoxically intensify desire and arousal. Purposefully delaying sexual activity for a designated period of time (days to weeks) while concurrently engaging in other activities that facilitates intimacy (e.g., more nonsexual physical contact, eye gazing, partaking of novel experiences) can resurrect passion.

The Limits of Sexual Enrichment

The partners in a male couple note a decline in their desire for each other. They have no interest in ending their relationship, but they also cannot ignore the fact that they are increasingly attracted to other men. They voluntarily partake of relationship therapy to resolve issues that are evident and they participate in sexual enrichment exercises, including sensate focus, monitoring and dissipating distracting thoughts, and learning to communicate about their sexual desires. They even try to manipulate their dopamine levels by engaging in new activities, making physical contact as often as possible, and even engaging in sex when desire is missing. These interventions have indeed proven that they love each other and have no wish to separate, but sexual desire and passion have only marginally improved. What is going on here?

Sexual desire disorders are the most intractable of all sexual problems; there is no simple solution to establishing or reestablishing sexual desire for one's partner. If sexual desire is hidden beneath years of hurt, misunderstanding, and conflict, the goal is to eradicate these distractions and clutter so as to expose the hidden desire. At the individual level, by freeing ourselves of our internalized restraints, we too can allow desire to flourish. Still, if a man truly no longer has desire for his partner, if it is not merely suppressed beneath an untold number of personal and relationship issues, the chances of sparking desire is not probable. To quote William Maurice in his review of sexual desire in men, "[I]t is so very difficult to alter the quantity of a man's sexual interest" (2007, p. 209).

The human brain inevitably eases the clamor of passion seen in the early stages of a relationship. There are several possible ways this can occur. The brain can begin to produce less of the neurochemicals, such as dopamine, associated with passion. Receptors for these same chemicals may become desensitized. Or, finally, our brain pumps out other chemicals that counteract the effects of the neurochemistry of raw lust. There is evidence for all three, and it is quite possible that all play a role. Regardless of how our brain adapts to the chemistry of passion, feelings of lust and arousal for our partners begin to recede. Sexual enrichment exercises may lead to a short-term and temporary rise in these neurochemicals, but they will quickly dissipate. The only foolproof way to recapture that level of sexual intensity for an extended period of time is to fall in love with another person. We simply do not have a method of increasing substantial long-term sexual desire and passion for our partners.

Regardless, the acknowledged limitations of sexual enrichment do not negate the value of the many interventions presented in this chapter. What sexual enrichment exercises and couples counseling do successfully achieve is an increase in both attachment and intimacy between partners. Men who participate in these interventions will come to appreciate each other, have a better understanding of each other, and even grow to love each other more. Sexual desire may move incrementally in the right direction, but commitment and love will soar to new heights. And many couples would accept this as a successful outcome. Sex researchers Bob Berkowitz and Susan Yager-Berkowitz, for example, find that many couples are "satisfied in every room of the house except the bedroom. Perhaps they have made peace with the fact that their marriage is without passion but not without love, and that is considered to be fair exchange."

But is this enough? For some couples, even temporarily, this might suffice. Others are not so obliging in living with an absence of sexual excitement. And for these latter couples, it's time to begin that uncomfortable dialogue about non-monogamy.

Afterword

IN THE INTRODUCTION to this book, I proposed that strict long-term monogamy for gay male couples is improbable. My research for this text leads me to this same conclusion. I am certain that there are couples out there that have maintained long-term monogamy for years into decades, but the research does indicate that these couples will be a minority. I won't deny the existence of studies that do find male couples achieving monogamy, but they always lead me to question just how truthful and candid these men are during their interviews regarding additional sexual activity. Also, I question how long these couples have been together. We have amassed sufficient evidence to determine that in the first two years of a relationship, sexual exclusivity is prized. Thus a study that has a large number of couples in the early stages of a relationship will skew the results to support a monogamy hypothesis. All in all, when we compare the results of animal studies, anthropological endeavors, theories of human evolution and adaptation, and current research in human sexuality, the penchant for nonmonogamy is hard to contest.

Recognizing that infidelity ranks as a dominant reason for divorce and separation across the globe, a rational response would be to question whether long-term monogamy is actually possible based on such statistics. Rarely however is such a question proffered; infidelity instead is labeled a transgression and blame is dispersed to miscreant individuals, as the unfortunate outcome of unaddressed relationship conflict, or to increasing societal permissiveness. Expectations and beliefs about the morality of monogamy, long accepted as true, invaluable, and worthy of our aspirations, are taken for granted even when evidence to the contrary surrounds us. In her examination of infidelity across the globe, Pamela Druckerman discovered, "Most Americans who discover a partner's affair become determined to get back into a monogamous situation, either with the same person or someone new. Couples therapy, long conversations, and even divorce are all meant to restore monogamy. American's don't lose their faith in fidelity even after fidelity fails them in practice" (2007, p. 133).

There is of course no logical reason to place monogamy at the top of a hierarchy of evidence of commitment. Two men pooling their resources to buy a house together is ample proof of commitment, but for many gay men, this would still be secondary to monogamy. One client I worked with stayed by his partner after a traumatic automobile accident that forever changed both their lives. Instead of a mutual couple, one was now a caretaker. And he followed through on his responsibilities with little complaint and much devotion, including learning to give injections, packing bedsores, and changing jobs so as to have more freedom to attend medical appointments. If this isn't commitment, what is? Friends repeatedly told him that they themselves would never be able to do what he was doing and that his partner was oh so fortunate to have him in his life. Still, when it was discovered that this same male was engaging in occasional anonymous sex on the side, all other evidence of commitment was nullified. Monogamy seems to trump all and is accepted by so many gay men as the only accepted valid signifier of commitment and love.

In 1969, Carl Wittman wrote his "Gay Manifesto" that promulgated the idea that marriagelike relationships were the antithesis of what gay men should be seeking. He believed that our relationships should *not* be sexually exclusive, should *not* make promises about the future, and should *not* dictate inflexible roles. Over the last several decades contingents of gay men have vehemently fought against sexual exclusivity, though not necessarily because they believed long-term monogamy was impossible; instead they rallied against it simply because it reeked of heterosexual hegemony. Gay diatribes speak of sexual non-exclusivity as a model for relationships in the future— still, the suggested substitutions invariably present with their own set of problems that can create as much discontentment and fallibility as the paradigm they hope to surpass.

In the end, what does this all signify? No relationship configuration is necessarily and intrinsically better than another. There is no one relationship style that trumps all other no matter how persistently society inculcates the ideal of monogamy. Monogamy may be perfect for some couples for an extended period of time, maybe even a lifetime. For others, it will never be an option. And for the majority, this desire will ebb and flow. What is important is that couples expect and accept these shifting desires, explore their relevance and meanings for both men, and commit to working together to find a solution that accommodates these sometimes inexplicable changes in lust and passion. We should not hold steady to our belief that monogamy is supreme because society and history tells us that it is supreme. Simply scratching the façade of history instead informs us just the contrary.

And as we acknowledge the impermanence of monogamy in relationships, we must also concede that a lack of sexual exclusivity does not indicate that our relationship is moribund or, less extreme, faltering. Cultural studies indicate that across the globe discovered infidelity hurts the betrayed partner; it is indeed painful. But other cultures do not deem it as a significant indicator that a relationship is in trouble. In the same study mentioned above, Pamela Druckerman found that other cultures did not treat infidelity "like a foreign invader that needs to be eradicated, but more like a fact of life" (p. 110). Michael LaSala, who I believe is the most knowledgeable expert in the country on gay male monogamy, iterated a similar conclusion: We have little understanding of the link between monogamy and relationship commitment for gay men from different ethnic and cultural groups. Maybe infidelity is understood as having less valence for a gay male relationship dependent on one's culture?

Infidelity may be the tip of the iceberg in regards to systemic, long-standing, and mutually destructive relationship problems, or it could be the outcome of a sexual opportunity in which belief about the sanctity of monogamy temporarily cedes to a neurochemically primed sexual arousal. Infidelity can signify much, but it can also mean very little in regards to commitment to our current relationship. The myth of monogamy requires us to believe that infidelity is tantamount to a crisis. And indeed, sometimes infidelity is a crisis, but certainly not every time.

Monogamy is a worthy aspiration for many couples. Just remember that several years from now, we may change our minds. And though the future may offer different sexual and relationships scripts to follow, particularly those that hopefully help men better achieve satisfaction simultaneously as a couple and as individuals, we will still always be drawn to both monogamy and sexual freedom. Which one wins out changes from day to day.

REFERENCES

Ali, L., & Miller, L. (2004). The secret lives of wives. *Newsweek*, 2, 46–54.

Allan, G. (2004). Being unfaithful: His and her affairs. In J. Duncombe, K. Harrison, G. Allan, & D. Marsden (Eds.), *The State of Affairs* (pp. 121–140). Mahwah, NJ: Lawrence Erlbaum Associates.

Alonzo, D. (2005). Working with same-sex couples. In M. Harway (Ed.), *Handbook of Couples Therapy* (370–385). Hoboken, NJ: John Wiley & Sons.

Atwood, J. (2005). Cyber-affairs: "What's the big deal?" therapeutic considerations. In F. Piercy, K. Hertlein, & J. Wetchler (Eds.), *Handbook of the Clinical Treatment of Infidelity* (pp. 117–134). New York: Haworth Press.

Banfield, S., & McCabe, M. (2001). Extra relationship involvement among women: Are they different from men? *Archives of Sexual Behavior, 30*, 119–142.

Barash, D., & Lipton, J. (2001). *The Myth of Monogamy*. New York: W.H. Freeman and Company.

Baumeister, R., Maner, J., & DeWall, N. (2006). Theories of human sexuality. In R. McAnulty & M. Burnette (Eds.), *Sex and Sexuality Volume I* (pp. 17–34). Westport, CT: Praeger.

Baumeister, R., & Stillman, T. (2006). Erotic plasticity: Nature, culture, gender, and sexuality. In R. McAnulty & M. Burnette (Eds.), *Sex and Sexuality Volume I* (pp. 343–359). Westport, CT: Praeger.

Bay-Cheng, L. (2006). The social construction of sexuality: Religion, medicine, media, schools, and families. In R. McAnulty & M. Burnette (Eds.), *Sex and Sexuality Volume I* (pp. 203–228). Westport, CT: Praeger.

Bergling, T. (2007). *Chasing Adonis.* New York: Harrington Park Press.

Berzon, B. (2004). *Permanent Partners.* New York: Plume.

Bettinger, M. (2005). A family systems approach to working with sexually open gay male couples. In F. Piercy, K. Hertlein, & J. Wetchler (Eds.), *Handbook of the Clinical Treatment of Infidelity* (pp. 149–160). New York: Haworth Press.

Bianchi-Demicheli, F., & Zutter, A. (2005). Intensive short-term dynamic sex therapy: A proposal. *Journal of Sex & Marital Therapy, 31,* 57–72.

Blackmore, S. (1999). *The Meme Machine.* New York: Oxford University Press.

Blow, A. (2005). Face it head on: Helping a couple move through the painful and pernicious effects of infidelity. In F. Piercy, K. Hertlein, & J. Wetchler (Eds.), *Handbook of the Clinical Treatment of Infidelity* (pp. 91–102). New York: Haworth Press.

Blum, D. (1997). *Sex on the brain: The biological differences between men and women.* New York: Viking Press.

Bogaert, A., & Fawcett, C. (2006). Sexual desire issues and problems. In R. McAnulty & M. Burnette (Eds.), *Sex and Sexuality Volume II* (pp. 115–134). Westport, CT: Praeger.

Boyle, P., & Moore, J. (2007). Abstinence ed's nightmare. *Youth Today,* 16, 1.

Bradford, A., & Meston, C. (2007). The role of the brain and nervous system. In A. Fuglsang Owens & M. Tepper (Eds.), *Sexual Health* (pp. 17–42). Westport, CT: Praeger.

Brooks, G. (1997). The centerfold syndrome. In R. Levant & G. Brooks (Eds.), *Men and Sex* (pp. 28–57). New York: John Wiley & Sons.

Brown, E. (2001). *Patterns of Infidelity and Their Treatment.* Philadelphia, PA: Brunner-Routledge.

Brown, E. (2005). Split self affairs and their treatment. In F. Piercy, K. Hertlein, & J. Wetchler (Eds.), *Handbook of the Clinical Treatment of Infidelity* (pp. 55–69). New York: Haworth Press.

Buss, D. (1994). *The Evolution of Desire.* New York: Basic Books.

Buss, D. (2000). The evolution of happiness. *American Psychologist,* 55, 15–23.

Buss, D. (2000). *The Dangerous Passion: Why Jealousy Is as Necessary as Love and Sex.* New York: Free Press.

Buss, D. & Schmitt, D. (1993). Sexual strategies theory: An evolutionary perspective on human mating. *Psychology Review,* 100, 204–232.

Buunk, B., & Dijkstra, P. (2004). Men, women, and infidelity: Sex differences in extradyadic sex and jealousy. In J. Duncombe, K. Harrison, G. Allan, & D. Marsden (Eds.), *The State of Affairs* (pp. 103–120). Mahwah, NJ: Lawrence Erlbaum Associates.

Case, B. (2005). Healing the wounds of infidelity through the healing power of apology and forgiveness. In F. Piercy, K. Hertlein, & J. Wetchler (Eds.), *Handbook of the Clinical Treatment of Infidelity* (pp. 41–54). New York: Haworth Press.

Chernin, J. (2006). *Get Closer.* New York: Alyson Books.

Clark, R., & Hatfield, E. (1989).Gender differences in receptivity to sexual offers. *Journal of Psychology and Human Sexuality,* 2, 39–55.

Coleman, E., & Reece, R. (1988). Treating low sexual desire

among gay men. In S. Leiblum & R. Rosen (Eds.), *Sexual Desire Disorders* (pp. 413–445). New York: Guilford Press.

Davis D. L, & Whitten, R. G. (1987). The cross-cultural study of human sexuality. *Annual Review of Anthropology,* 16, 69–98.

Demakis, G. (2006). Sex and the brain. In R. McAnulty & M. Burnette (Eds.), *Sex and Sexuality Volume II* (pp. 19–36). Westport, CT: Praeger.

Denman, C. (2004). *Sexuality: A Biopsychosocial Approach.* New York: Palgrave Macmillan.

Druckerman, P. (2007). *Lust in Translation.* New York: Penguin.

Duncombe, J., & Marsden, D. (2004). "From here to epiphany . . .": Power and identity in the narrative of an affair. In J. Duncombe, K. Harrison, G. Allan, & D. Marsden (Eds.), *The State of Affairs.* (pp. 141–165). Mahwah, NJ: Lawrence Erlbaum Associates.

Dunkle, J. (1994). Counseling gay male clients: A review of treatment efficacy research: 1975–present. *Journal of Gay & Lesbian Psychotherapy,* 2, 1–19.

Febbraro, G. (2006). Sexual arousal disorders. In R. McAnulty & M. Burnette (Eds.), *Sex and Sexuality Volume II* (pp. 135–151). Westport, CT: Praeger.

Firestone, R., Firestone, L., & Catlett, J. (2006). *Sex and Love in*

Intimate Relationships. Washington, D.C.: American Psychological Association.

Fisher, B., Graham, K., & Duffecy, J. (2006). Chronic disease, disability, and sexuality. In R. McAnulty & M. Burnette (Eds.), *Sex and Sexuality Volume II* (pp. 233–260) Westport, CT: Praeger.

Fisher, H. (2004). *Why We Love.* New York: Henry Holt and Company.

Fitness, J. (2001). Betrayal, rejection, revenge, and forgiveness: An interpersonal script approach. In M. Leary (Ed.), *Interpersonal Rejection* (pp. 73–103). New York: Oxford University Press.

Geary, D. (2006). An evolutionary perspective on sexual and intimate relationships. In R. McAnulty & M. Burnette (Eds.), *Sex and Sexuality Volume II* (pp. 67–86). Westport, CT: Praeger.

George, K. (2000). *Mr. Right Is Out There.* New York: Alyson Books.

George, K. (2004). *Keeping Mr. Right.* New York: Alyson Books.

Giddens, A. (1992). *The Transformation of Intimacy.* Stanford, CA: Stanford University Press.

Gil-Rivas, V., & Kooyman, L. (2006). Sexual risk-taking:

Correlates and prevention. In R. McAnulty & M. Burnette (Eds.), *Sex and Sexuality Volume I* (pp. 321–342). Westport, CT: Praeger

Glass, S. & Wright, T. (1985). Sex differences in the type of extramarital involvement and marital dissatisfaction. *Sex Roles,* 12, 1101–1119.

Glass, S. & Wright, T. (1992). Justification for extramarital relationships: The association between attitudes, behaviors, and gender. *Journal of Sex Research,* 29, 361–387.

Good, G., & Sherrod, N. (1997). Men's resolution of nonrelational sex across the lifespan. In R. Levant & G. Brooks (Eds.), *Men and Sex* (pp. 181–204). New York: John Wiley & Sons.

Gorney, R. (2007). Evolution and the adaptive significance of asexual, sexual, and erotic touch. In M. Tepper & A. Fuglsang Owens (Eds.), *Sexual Health* (pp. 67–94). Westport, CT: Praeger.

Greenan, D., & Tunnell, G. (2003). *Couple Therapy with Gay Men.* New York: Guilford Press.

Harrison, K. (2004). The role of female friends in the management of affairs. In J. Duncombe, K. Harrison, G. Allan, & D. Marsden (Eds.), *The State of Affairs* (pp. 203–222). Mahwah, NJ: Lawrence Erlbaum Associates.

Hatfield, E., & Rapson, R. (2007). Love and sexual health. In

M. Tepper & A. Fuglsang Owens (Eds.), *Sexual Health* (pp. 43–66). Westport, CT: Praeger.

Heaphy, B., Donovan, C., & Weeks, J. (2004). A different affair? Openness and nonmonogamy in same sex relationships. In J. Duncombe, K. Harrison, G. Allan, & D. Marsden (Eds.), *The State of Affairs* (pp. 167–186). Mahwah, NJ: Lawrence Erlbaum Associates.

Herek, G. (2006). Legal recognition of same-sex relationships in the United States. *American Psychologist,* 61, 607–621.

Herlihy, D. (1995). Biology and history: The triumph of monogamy. *Journal of Interdisciplinary History,* 25, 571–583.

Hernandez, G. (2006, June 6). Big gay love. *The Advocate,* June, 36–42.

Hertlein, K., & Skaggs, G. (2005). Assessing the relationship between differentiation and infidelity: A structural equation model. In F. Piercy, K. Hertlein, & J. Wetchler (Eds.), *Handbook of the Clinical Treatment of Infidelity* (pp. 195–213). New York: Haworth Press.

Iasenza, S. (2006). Low sexual desire in gay, lesbian, and heterosexual peer marriages. In J. Scharff & D. Scharff (Eds.), *New Paradigms for Treating Relationships* (pp. 375–383). Lanham, Maryland: Jason Aronson.

Immerman, R., & Mackey, W. (1999). The societal dilemma of

multiple sexual partners: The costs of the loss of pair-bonding. *Marriage & Family Review*, 29, 3–19.

Isensee, R. (1996). *Love Between Men*. Los Angeles, CA: Alyson Press.

Jamieson, L. (2004). Intimacy, negotiated nonmonogamy, and the limits of the couple. In J. Duncombe, K. Harrison, G. Allan, & D. Marsden (Eds.), *The State of Affairs* (pp. 35–57). Mahwah, NJ: Lawrence Erlbaum Associates.

Joannides, P. (2007). Sex in America: From below the Victorian belt to the start of modern dating. In M. Tepper & A. Fugslang Owens (Eds.), *Sexual Health* (pp. 97–140). Westport, CT: Praeger.

Johnston, J. (1997). Appearance obsession: Women's reaction to men's objectification of their bodies. In R. Levant & G. Brooks (Eds.), *Men and Sex* (pp. 61–83). New York: John Wiley & Sons.

Johnson, S. (2005). Broken bonds: An emotionally focused approach to infidelity. In F. Piercy, K. Hertlein, & J. Wetchler (Eds.), *Handbook of the Clinical Treatment of Infidelity* (pp. 17–29). New York: Haworth Press.

Johnson, S. (2005). Your cheatin' heart: Myths and absurdities about extradyadic relationships. In F. Piercy, K. Hertlein, & J. Wetchler (Eds.), *Handbook of the Clinical Treatment of Infidelity* (pp. 161–172). New York: Haworth Press.

REFERENCES

Jordan, M. (2005). *Blessing Same-Sex Unions.* Chicago: University of Chicago Press.

Kanazawa, S., & Still, M. (1999). Why monogamy? *Social Forces,* 78, 25–50.

Kantor, M. (2005). *Together Forever: The Gay Man's Guide to Lifelong Love.* Naperville, IL: Sourcebooks Casablanca.

Kelly, J., & Kalichman, S. (1995). Increased attention to human sexuality can improve HIV-AIDS prevention efforts: Key research issues and directions. *Journal of Consulting and Clinical Psychology,* 63, 907–918.

Knapp, J. (1976). An exploratory study of seventeen sexually open marriages. *The Journal of Sex Research,* 12, 206–219.

Komisaruk, B., Beyer-Flores, C., & Whipple, B. (2006). *The Science of Orgasm.* Baltimore, MD: Johns Hopkins University Press.

Kontula, O., & Haavio-Mannila, E. (2004). Renaissance of romanticism in the era of increasing individualism. In J. Duncombe, K. Harrison, G. Allan, & D. Marsden (Eds.), *The State of Affairs* (pp. 79–102). Mahwah, NJ: Lawrence Erlbaum Associates.

LaSala, M. (2001). Monogamous or not: Understanding and counseling gay male couples. *Families in Society.*

LaSala, M. (2004). Extradyadic sex and gay male couples:

REFERENCES

Comparing monogamous and nonmonogamous relationships. *Families in Society.*

LaSala, M. (2004). Monogamy of the heart: Extradyadic sex and gay male couples. *Journal of Gay & Lesbian Social Services, 17*, 1–24.

Lazarus, A. (1988). A multimodal perspective on problems of sexual desire. In S. Leiblum & R. Rosen (Eds.), *Sexual Desire Disorders* (pp. 145–167). New York: Guilford Press.

Leedes, R. (2007). Compulsive or other problematic sexual behavior. In A. Fuglsang Owens & M. Tepper (Eds.), *Sexual Health Volume 4* (pp. 365–381). Westport, CT: Praeger.

Leiblum, S., & Rosen, R. (1988). Introduction: Changing perspectives on sexual desire. In S. Leiblum & R. Rosen (Eds.), *Sexual Desire Disorders* (pp. 1–17). New York: Guilford Press.

Levant, R. (1997). Nonrelational sexuality in men. In R. Levant & G. Brooks (Eds.), *Men and Sex* (pp. 9–27). New York: John Wiley & Sons.

Levant, R., & Brooks, G. (1997). *Men and Sex.* New York: John Wiley & Sons.

Levine, S. (1988). Intrapsychic and individual aspects of sexual desire. In S. Leiblum & R. Rosen (Eds.), *Sexual Desire Disorders* (pp. 21–44). New York: Guilford Press.

Levinger, G. (1976). A social psychological perspective on marital dissolution. *Journal of Social Issues, 32,* 21–47.

Litzinger, S., & Coop Gordon, K. (2005). Exploring relationships among communication, sexual satisfaction, and marital satisfaction. *Journal of Sex & Marital Therapy, 31,* 409–424.

LoPiccolo, J., & Friedman, J. (1988). Broad-spectrum treatment of low sexual desire: Integration of cognitive, behavioral, and systemic therapy. In S. Leiblum & R. Rosen (Eds.), *Sexual Desire Disorders* (pp. 107–144). New York: Guilford Press.

Lusterman, D. (2005). Marital infidelity: The effects of delayed traumatic reaction. In F. Piercy, K. Hertlein, & J. Wetchler (Eds.), *Handbook of the Clinical Treatment of Infidelity* (pp. 71–81). New York: Haworth Press.

Lusterman, D. (1998). *Infidelity.* Oakland, CA: New Harbinger Publications.

Lusterman, D. (1997). Repetitive infidelity, womanizing, and Don Juanism. In R. Levant & G. Brooks (Eds.), *Men and Sex* (pp. 84–99). New York: John Wiley & Sons.

Marcus U., Bremer V., Hamouda O., et al. (2006). Understanding recent increases in the incidence of sexually transmitted infections in men having sex with men: Changes in risk behavior from risk avoidance to risk reduction. *Sexually Transmitted Diseases, 33,* 11–7.

Martell, C., Safren, S., & Prince, C. (2004). *Cognitive-Behavioral Therapies with Lesbian, Gay, and Bisexual Clients.* New York: Guilford Press.

Maurice, W. (2007). Sexual desire disorders in men. In S. Leiblum (Ed.), *Principles and Practice of Sex Therapy* (pp. 181–211). New York: Guilford Press.

McCarthy, B., & Fucito, L. (2005). Integrating medication, realistic expectations, and therapeutic interventions in the treatment of male sexual dysfunction. *Journal of Sex & Marital Therapy, 31,* 319–328.

Melotti, U. (1981). Towards a new theory of the origin of the family. *Current Anthropology,* 22, 625–630.

Miller, N. (2006). *Out of the past.* New York: Alyson Books.

Mitchell, S. (2002). *Can love last?* New York: Norton.

Moore, J. (2007). In the mood for evidence. *Youth Today,* 16, 26.

Morell, V. (1998). A new look at monogamy. *Science, 281,* 1982–1983.

Morgan, D. (2004). The sociological significance of affairs. In J. Duncombe, K. Harrison, G. Allan, & D. Marsden (Eds.), *The State of Affairs* (pp. 15–34). Mahwah, NJ: Lawrence Erlbaum Associates.

Moultrup, D. (2005). Undercurrents. In F. Piercy, K. Hertlein, & J. Wetchler (Eds.), *Handbook of the Clinical Treatment of Infidelity* (pp. 31–40). New York: Haworth Press.

Murray, S. (1997). Explaining away same-sex sexualities. *Anthropology Today,* 13, 2–5.

Nelson, T., Piercy, F., & Sprenkle, D. (2005). Internet infidelity: A multi-phase delphi study. In F. Piercy, K. Hertlein, & J. Wetchler (Eds.), *Handbook of the Clinical Treatment of Infidelity* (pp. 173–194). New York: Haworth Press.

Newton, E. (1993). My best informant's dress: The erotic equation is fieldwork.

Cultural Anthropology, 8, 3–23.

Nichols, M., & Shernoff, M. (2007). Therapy with sexual minorities. In S. Leiblum (Ed.), *Principles and Practice of Sex Therapy* (pp. 379–415). New York: Guilford Press.

Overall, C. (1998). Monogamy, nonmonogamy, and identity. *Hypatia,* 13, 1–17.

Peplau, L., Cochran, S., & Mays, V. (1997). A national survey of the intimate relationships of African American lesbians and gay men. In B Greene (Ed.), *Ethnic and Cultural Diversity among Lesbians and Gay Men* (pp. 11–38). Thousand Oaks, CA: Sage Publications.

Perel. E. (2006). *Mating in Captivity.* New York: HarperCollins.

Peterman, T., Heffelfinger, J., Swint, E., et al. (2005). The changing epidemiology of syphilis. *Sexually Transmitted Diseases,* 32, S4–S10.

Pinker, S. (1997). *How the Mind Works.* New York: Norton.

Pittman, F., & Pittman Wagers, T. (2005). The relationship, if any, between marriage and infidelity. In F. Piercy, K. Hertlein, & J. Wetchler (Eds.), *Handbook of the Clinical Treatment of Infidelity* (pp. 135–148). New York: Haworth Press.

Potts, M., & Short, R. (1999). *Ever Since Adam and Eve.* New York: Cambridge University Press.

Reece, M., Dodge, B., & McBride, K. (2006). Sexual compulsivity: Issues and challenges. In R. McAnulty & M. Burnette (Eds.), *Sex and Sexuality Volume II* (pp. 213–232). Westport, CT: Praeger.

Regan, P. (2006). Love. In R. McAnulty & M. Burnette (Eds.), *Sex and Sexuality Volume II* (pp. 87–114). Westport, CT: Praeger.

Rice, C. (2005, March 29). Monogamy and me. *The Advocate.*

Rosen, R., &. Leiblum, S. (1988). A sexual scripting approach to problems of desire. In S. Leiblum & R. Rosen (Eds.), *Sexual Desire Disorders* (pp. 168–191). New York: Guilford Press.

Rotello, G. (1997). *Sexual Ecology: AIDS and the Destiny of Gay Men.* New York: Dutton.

Roughgarden, J. (2004). *Evolution's Rainbow.* Berkeley, CA: University of California Press.

Rowland, D. (2006). The psychobiology of sexual arousal and

response: Physical and psychological factors that control our sexual response. In R. McAnulty & M. Burnette (Eds.), *Sex and Sexuality Volume II* (pp. 37–66). Westport, CT: Praeger.

Satterly, B., & Dyson,D. (2007). Sexual identities of gay men and lesbians: Cultural foundations and controversies. In M. Tepper & A. Fuglsang Owens (Eds.), *Sexual Health* (pp. 315–342). Westport, CT: Praeger.

Savage, D. (2007, November 7–13). Savage love. *Philadelphia Weekly,* p. 78.

Scasta, D. (1998). Moving from coming out to intimacy. *Journal of Gay & Lesbian Psychotherapy,* 2, 99–111.

Scheinkman, M. (2005). Beyond the trauma of betrayal: Reconsidering affairs in couples therapy. *Family Process,* 44, 227–244.

Schiemann, J., & Smith, W. (1996). The homosexual couple. In H. Kessler & I. Yalom (Eds.), *Treating Couples* (pp. 97–136). San Francisco, CA: Jossey-Bass.

Schwartz, B. (2000). Self-determination: The tyranny of freedom. *American Psychologist,* 55, 79–88.

Schwartz, M., & Masters, W. (1988). Inhibited sexual desire: The Masters and Johnson Insitute treatment model. In S. Leiblum & R. Rosen (Eds.), *Sexual Desire Disorders* (pp. 229–242). New York: Guilford Press.

Schwartz, P., & Rutter, V. (1998). *The Gender of Sexuality.* Thousand Oaks, CA: Pine Forge Press.

Scrivner, R. (1997). Gay men and nonrelational sex. In R. Levant & G. Brooks (Eds.), *Men and Sex* (pp. 229–256). New York: John Wiley & Sons.

Sexuality Information and Education Council of the United States (2004). *Guidelines for Comprehensive Sexuality Education.* New York.

Shackelford, T., & Buss, D. (1997). Cues to infidelity. *Personality and Social Psychology Bulletin, 23,* 1034–1045.

Shernoff, M. (2006). Negotiated nonmonogamy and male couples. *Family Process,* 45, 407–418.

Shibley Hyde, J. (1996). Where are the gender differences? Where are the gender similarities? In D. Buss & N. Malamuth (Eds.), *Sex, Power, Conflict* (pp. 107–118). New York: Oxford University Press.

Slater, L. (2006). True love. *National Geographic,* 209, 32–49.

Slowinski, J. (2007). Psychological and relationship aspects of male sexuality. In A. Fuglsang Owens & M. Tepper (Eds.), *Sexual Health Volume 4* (pp. 15–46). Westport, CT: Praeger.

Smith, T. (2006). Sexual behavior in the United States. In R. McAnulty & M. Burnette (Eds.),. *Sex and Sexuality Volume I* (pp. 103–132). Westport, CT: Praeger.

Sonenschein, D. (1966). Homosexuality as a subject of anthropological inquiry.

Anthropological Quarterly, 39, 73–82.

Spitalnick, J., & McNair, L. (2005). Couples therapy with gay and lesbian clients: An analysis of important clinical issues. *Journal of Sex & Marital Therapy, 31,* 43–56.

Stalfa, F., & Hastings, C. (2005). "Accusatory suffering" in the offended spouse. In F. Piercy, K. Hertlein, & J. Wetchler (Eds.), *Handbook of the Clinical Treatment of Infidelity.* (pp. 83–90). New York: Haworth Press.

Stayton, W. (2007). Sexual value systems and sexual health. In M. Tepper & A. Fuglsang Owens (Eds.), *Sexual Health.* (pp. 79– 96). Westport, CT: Praeger.

Stock, W. (1997). Sex as commodity: Men and the sex industry. In R. Levant & G. Brooks (Eds.), *Men and Sex* (pp. 100–132). New York: John Wiley & Sons.

Strong, B., DeVault, C., Sayad, B., & Yarber, W. (2005). *Human Sexuality.* New York: McGraw-Hill.

Symons, D. (1979). *The Evolution of Human Sexuality.* New York: Oxford University Press.

Tepper, M. (2007). Systems that contribute to sexual response and expression. In A. Fuglsang Owens & M. Tepper (Eds.), *Sexual Health* (pp. 1–16). Westport, CT: Praeger.

Tepper, M., & Fuglsang, Owens, A. (2007). Current controversies in sexual health: Sexual addictions and compulsion. In A. Fuglsang Owens & M. Tepper (Eds.), *Sexual Health Volume 4* (pp. 349–363). Westport, CT: Praeger.

Vandervoort, L., & Duck, S. (2004). Sex, lies, and transformation. In J. Duncombe, K. Harrison, G. Allan, & D. Marsden (Eds.), *The State of Affairs* (pp. 1–13.). Mahwah, NJ: Lawrence Erlbaum Associates.

Vangelisti, A., & Gerstenberger, M. (2004). Communication and marital infidelity. In J. Duncombe, K. Harrison, G. Allan, & D. Marsden (Eds.), *The State of Affairs* (pp. 59–78). Mahwah, NJ: Lawrence Erlbaum Associates.

Verhulst, J., & Heiman, J. (1988). A systems perspective on sexual desire. In S. Leiblum & R. Rosen (Eds.), *Sexual Desire Disorders* (pp. 243–267). New York: Guilford Press.

Weston, K. (1993). Lesbian/Gay studies in the house of anthropology. *Annual Review of Anthropology, 22,* 339–367.

White, E. (1998, June 23). What century is this anyway? *The Advocate.*

White, D. & Burton, M. (1988). Causes of polygyny: Ecology, economy, kinship, and warfare. *American Anthropologist, 90,* 871–887.

Whitty, M., & Carr, A. (2005). Taking the good with the bad:

Applying Klein's work to further our understandings of cyber-cheating. In F. Piercy, K. Hertlein, & J. Wetchler (Eds.), *Handbook of the Clinical Treatment of Infidelity* (pp. 103–115). New York: Haworth Press.

Wieder, J. (1998, June 23). Meditations on monogamy—spiritual guru Deepak Chopra interview. *The Advocate.*

Wincze, J., & Carey, M. (2001). *Sexual Dysfunction.* New York: Guilford Press.

Wittenberger, J., & Tilson, R. (1980). The evolution of monogamy: Hypotheses and evidence. *Annual Review of Ecology and Systematics,* 11, 197–232.

Woog, D. (1998, June 23). One on one: Homosexual monogamy. *The Advocate.*

Zilbergeld, B. (1999). *The New Male Sexuality.* New York: Bantam Books.

Zimbardo, P.G., Maslach, C., & C. Haney. (2000). Reflections on the Stanford Prison

Experiment Genesis, transformations, consequences. In T. Blass (Ed.), *Current perspectives on the Milgram paradigm.* NJ: Erlbaum.